Also by Natalie Cole

Angel on My Shoulder: An Autobiography (with Digby Diehl)

Also by David Ritz

BIOGRAPHIES

Divided Soul: The Life of Marvin Gaye
Faith in Time: The Life of Jimmy Scott

AUTOBIOGRAPHIES

Ray Charles: *Brother Ray*
Smokey Robinson: *Smokey: Inside My Life*
B.B. King: *Blues All Around Me*
Etta James: *Rage to Survive*
The Neville Brothers: *The Brothers*
Jerry Wexler: *Rhythm and the Blues*
Aretha Franklin: *Aretha: From These Roots*
Walter Yetnikoff: *Howling at the Moon*
Robert Guillaume: *Guillaume: A Life*
Laila Ali: *Reach!*
Gary Sheffield: *Inside Power*
Felicia "Snoop" Pearson: *Grace After Midnight*
Lang Lang: *Journey of a Thousand Miles*
Don Rickles: *Rickles' Book*
Jerry Leiber and Mike Stoller: *Hound Dog*
Paul Shaffer: *We'll Be Here for the Rest of Our Lives*
Grandmaster Flash: *The Adventures of Grandmaster Flash*
Tavis Smiley: *What I Know for Sure*
Cornel West: *Brother West: Living and Loving Out Loud*
Archbishop Carl Bean: *I Was Born This Way*

NOVELS

Search for Happiness
The Man Who Brought the Dodgers Back to Brooklyn
Blues Notes Under a Green Felt Hat
Barbells and Saxophones
Family Blood
Take It Off, Take It All Off!
Passion Flowers
Sanctified Blues (with Mable John)
Stay Out of the Kitchen (with Mable John)
Love Tornado (with Mable John)

INSPIRATIONAL

Messengers: Portraits of African American Ministers, Evangelists, Gospel Singers and Other Messengers of "the Word"

LOVE BROUGHT ME BACK

A Journey of Loss and Gain

NATALIE COLE

WITH DAVID RITZ

SIMON & SCHUSTER

NEW YORK LONDON TORONTO SYDNEY

Simon & Schuster
1230 Avenue of the Americas
New York, NY 10020

First Simon & Schuster hardcover edition November 2010

SIMON & SCHUSTER and colophon are registered trademarks of Simon & Schuster, Inc.

All photographs are from the author's collection.

For information about special discounts for bulk purchases, please contact Simon & Schuster Special Sales at 1-866-506-1949 or business@simonandschuster.com.

The Simon & Schuster Speakers Bureau can bring authors to your live event. For more information or to book an event, contact the Simon & Schuster Speakers Bureau at 1-866-248-3049 or visit our website at www.simonspeakers.com.

Designed by C. Linda Dingler

Manufactured in the United States of America

1 3 5 7 9 10 8 6 4 2

Library of Congress Cataloging-in-Publication Data
Cole, Natalie.
Love brought me back : a journey of loss and gain / Natalie Cole with David Ritz.
p. cm.
1. Cole, Natalie, 1950– —Health. 2. Kidneys—Transplantation—Patients—United States—Biography. 3. Cole, Carole, 1944–2009. 4. Karina, Jessica. 5. Argueta, Patty. I. Ritz, David. II. Title.
ML420.C636A3 2010
782.42164092—dc22
[B] 2010037433

ISBN 978-1-4516-0606-5
ISBN 978-1-4516-0607-2 (ebook)

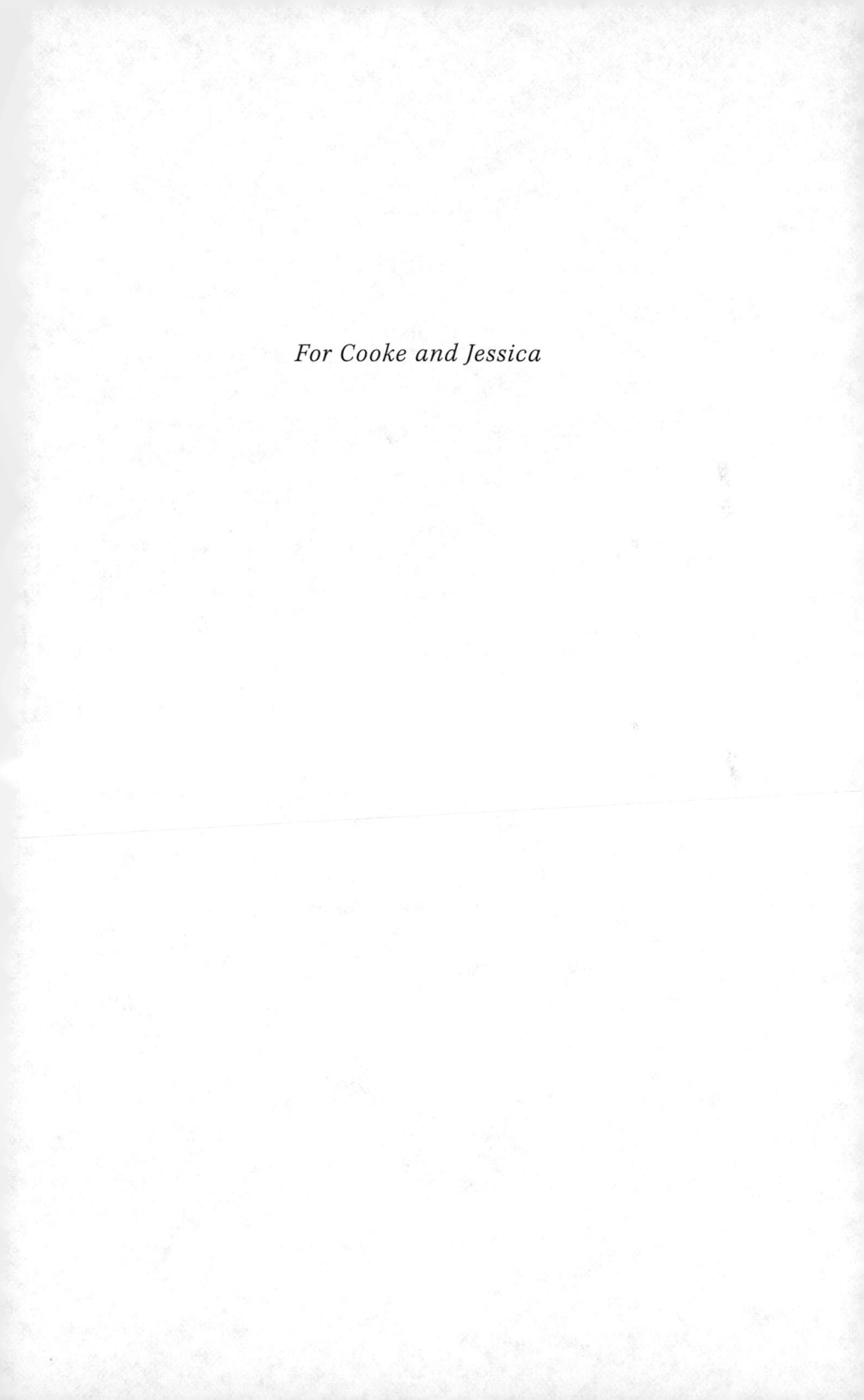

For Cooke and Jessica

Love Brought Me Back

1

I AM AMAZED that I am alive.

Given the crazy way that I lived my life, the chances I took, and the dangers I brought on, I should not be here. And yet, at age sixty, I sit at my desk, healthy and energetic, as I prepare to tell the remarkable story of these past two years.

I feel compelled to tell you this story because I believe that it will illustrate the goodness of a living God. I also tell it because I still need to process what happened to me and my sister, and to Jessica and Patty.

I see this story as the orchestration of four sisters whose

lives became intertwined in improbable and seemingly impossible ways.

It is a story of loss and gain.

I lost a loving sister named Cooke (pronounced "Cookie").

Patty lost a loving sister named Jessica.

Patty's loss gained me my life.

Cooke's spirit inspired my life, just as Jessica's shining spirit inspired Patty.

We are all joined together—not just Natalie, Cooke, Jessica, and Patty, but all humankind. Our dramas may seem separate, but my drama has brought me to an inescapable conclusion: that we are deeply and permanently connected.

Those connections are exquisite multifaceted pieces, like gems in a mosaic. When we study each piece, we are enthralled. When we step back to see the mosaic in its entirety—the big picture of our lives—we are awestruck.

I am awestruck. I am aware that it is only with God's grace that I am alive and able to tell this story.

2

New Year's Eve, 2007

I'M NO SQUARE—my friends will tell you that—and I love to party, but my favorite way to party on New Year's Eve is church, especially Faithful Central, the praise-and-worship congregation that took over the Forum, former home of the Los Angeles Lakers.

My whole crew accompanied me. My girlfriends Benita and Tammy were there, and so was my son, Robbie, who, at age thirty, showed, among other talents, his late father's great gift for preaching. My aunt Marie and uncle Kearney were also there, along with my friend Quaford, my brother from another mother.

I usually attend the Mt. Moriah Baptist Church in South Central L.A., a smaller and more intimate congregation, but on this night I wanted to experience the full-tilt gospel joy, the higher-than-high energy of Kurt Carr's magnificent choir, the heart-stopping rhythms and spine-tingling riffs of sacred singing. Along with thousands of fellow believers, I wanted to wave my arms and stomp my feet, feel that Holy Ghost power, and thank God for this past year and the year ahead, a year filled with so many possibilities and so much promise. After the services, I arrived back home in a state of spiritual renewal. I could not have been happier.

A good deal of my happiness came from the record I was making, *Still Unforgettable,* a follow-up to *Unforgettable . . . with Love,* the multi-Grammy-winning record that revitalized my career in 1990. *Unforgettable . . . with Love* was a beautiful and magical reunion with my father, who had died at age forty-six in 1965, nine days after my fifteenth birthday.

I've always adored my father's music, but ever since I'd started singing, whether it was while I was still a student at the University of Massachusetts or professionally, I avoided Dad's material. I was determined to create my own identity. My first hits, in fact, were straight-up rhythm and blues. My voice was compared to Aretha Franklin's, though, for my money, no one compares to Aretha. By the time I approached my forties, I had the self-assurance to approach all the genres I love so deeply: R & B, rock, jazz, and pop. My dad bridged jazz and pop with such aplomb that, even with my newfound confidence, I was hesitant. But I did it, and the result changed my musical life. *Unforgettable . . . with Love* sold some fourteen million copies.

Returning to the *Unforgettable* concept brought back the thrill of reuniting with my father in the recording studio. On the original album, through the miracle of modern engineering, I had sung with him on the title track. This time I wanted to try a different kind of song, not as melancholy as "Unforgettable," but upbeat and whimsical. So I chose "Walkin' My Baby Back Home." What could be sweeter?

Happily, my mind was on music. After two and a half unsuccessful marriages—two and a half because the third had recently ended in an annulment—romance was a distant concept. I was more than content to concentrate on family, friends, and career.

Following some preliminary work on the record in January, I scheduled a routine doctor's appointment in early February. I had a hernia that required minor surgery. So I went to my general practitioner, Dr. Maurice Levy, for blood work before the operation. He said he'd call only if there were any problems.

I was in the recording studio when, in fact, he did call.

"Natalie," he said. "Your blood's not normal. I want you to see a kidney specialist."

"Is it serious?"

"Can't tell at this point. But let's take every precaution."

I went to see the kidney specialist, Dr. Joel Mittleman, to whom I will be forever indebted. He took additional tests. When he called with the results, he sounded worried.

"It's hepatitis. You need to see a liver specialist."

Okay.

I took a deep breath and called my sister Cooke, my best friend.

"I have hepatitis," I said.

"Which kind?" asked Cooke, who was five years older than me and, as far as I'm concerned, knowledgeable about—well, just about everything. A great believer in homeopathy, Cooke advocated natural remedies.

"He didn't say what kind," I answered.

"Well, hepatitis comes in different flavors."

"He didn't say anything about chocolate, vanilla, or strawberry," I said, trying to keep things light.

"You'll be fine, Sweetie," Cooke assured me, using my family nickname. "Just call me after you see the liver man."

The liver man was Dr. Graham Woolf. I gave more blood, and he took more tests. He was a great guy—handsome and kind. But even with those wonderful qualities, he did not have good news. I sat in his office with that same lump in my throat. My stomach was doing flip-flops.

Fortunately, my close friends Benita Hill Johnson and

Tammy Engelstein were with me. It's bad enough to receive bad news. It's really bad when it comes from a doctor. I was deeply grateful for the presence of two of my dearest friends.

Dr. Woolf didn't beat around the bush. "Miss Cole," he said, "you have hepatitis C."

My heart sank. Hep C is a serious liver infection.

"How did I contract it?"

"It could have been a blood transfusion. A tattoo. Or a drug injection. Hepatitis C is not uncommon among intravenous drug users."

"I was an intravenous drug user," I said. "But it's been twenty-five-plus years."

"Back then," asked Dr. Woolf, "did you share needles with others?"

"All the time. I was on heroin."

"That might explain it."

"But, Doctor, I've been clean and sober ever since."

"The virus can remain dormant in your body for decades. Its manifestation is highly unpredictable. You never know when or if it's going to assault your liver."

"And all because of something I did a lifetime ago?"

"I'm afraid so."

I closed my eyes. I really didn't want to hear what I was hearing. I didn't want to know about it. Didn't want to accept it. Didn't want to see a scene that, for a few seconds, was playing out in my mind.

• • •

1975. I was twenty-five and had recorded my first album in Chicago. The initial single, "This Will Be (an Everlasting Love)," was starting to climb the charts. I had a small following from my club dates but was hardly a star. I was, in fact, a junkie. I had come to New York City to score dope. I was running up to Harlem to buy heroin. I wanted one thing and one thing only—the feeling I got when the shit shot through my veins. I was going to get it, no matter what. Billy Strayhorn said the A train is the quickest way to get to Harlem, so I took the A train. Jumped off at 125th Street and walked over to a run-down building.

I could walk the streets of Harlem undisturbed. I was comfortable in that neighborhood. I didn't have buddies up there, but people knew me as Nat's daughter. People welcomed me. Even the police knew who I was.

"Hey, Natalie, how you doin', baby?" an older man greeted me.

"Lookin' good, mama," said a young cat. "Lookin' *real* good."

Even as a junkie, I took pride in my appearance. I looked like I was ready to shop at Saks. I was obviously overdressed for an appointment with the dope man.

The dope man lived in a nasty brick building where he sold his wares to whoever had the bread. I had the bread and the nerve to walk down those dark hallways, filled with graffiti and stinking of urine, until I reached his apartment and loudly knocked.

"It's Natalie," I said.

"Good God almighty, you back already?"

And with that, the dope man opened the door, smiled, and invited me in.

A few minutes later, I floated out. On the radio from someone's porch in Harlem, I heard the strains of "This Will Be (an Everlasting Love)." All I could think of was an everlasting high.

"Natalie, I know this is difficult news for you to hear," said Dr. Woolf, taking me out of my flashback, "but treatment will be needed."

"What kind?"

"Interferon."

"My brother, Kelly, took interferon when he was sick with AIDS. It has devastating side effects, doesn't it?"

"The side effects are serious, but the treatment is necessary. Here's how it works. Interferon is a chemical that we all have in our bodies in very small amounts. It fights off viruses, but it's easily overwhelmed by certain viruses like hepatitis C. That's why you require additional interferon through weekly injections."

"Isn't that considered a form of chemotherapy?" I asked.

"Yes."

My sister Cooke, the naturalist, had been talking against chemotherapy for years.

"And if I don't start this chemotherapy?" I had to ask.

"You'll become very, very sick."

"And die?"

"At some point your liver will stop functioning."

"I'm in the middle of making a record. I simply can't stop now for treatments."

"The treatments don't need to start immediately. But soon. Very soon."

"There are other kinds of treatments," said Cooke, with whom I spoke every evening.

"Dr. Woolf claims chemotherapy is the most effective."

"Western prejudices, Western doctors, Western medicines concocted by profit-crazed Western pharmaceutical firms. Why not look into alternative programs?"

Cooke was Ms. Alternative, a hippie before the word existed. She was a bohemian, an actress, and a sweetheart. I adored Cooke. Carol Cooke Cole was my adopted sister. Her mom, who died of tuberculosis in 1949, was my mother's sister. Cooke's dad had died the year before, and my parents brought her to our home. Amid great controversy, my parents had moved to a mansion in Hancock Park, a super-WASPy section of Los Angeles populated by, among others, the governor of California, Earl Warren. Mom and

Dad broke the color barrier and, with the help of a letter from Eleanor Roosevelt, defied the nonwhite covenant and set up house. They had to endure the sight of crosses being burned on the front lawn. When the bigoted neighbors told Dad that they didn't want undesirables moving in, he said, "Neither do I. If I see any, I'll let you know."

When I made my grand entrance on February 6, 1950, Cooke was five and had been living with my parents only a few short months. Dad nicknamed her Cooke. The name came from his favorite comic strip; Dagwood and Blondie's daughter was named Cookie. To go with Cooke, Dad called me Sweetie. Everyone thought the name came from my love of sweets, but the real reason is that Dad wanted a linguistic match for Cooke.

I was Cooke's favorite playmate, her little doll. She was big sis—protective, smart, and hip from Jump Street.

We stuck together for many reasons. First, there was little-sis big-sis affection. I loved having an older sister to look up to, and in return, Cooke loved having a playmate to lead around. We also stuck together in emotional survival mode. Our mother, bless her heart, was distant. Dad was warm and cuddly, but Dad was on the road at least two-thirds of the time. Because Mom usually accompanied him, we were left with the maids and nannies and Mom's super-cool sister, Aunt Charlotte.

Dad always wanted a boy, and when I was nine, my parents adopted my brother, Kelly. Two years later, Mom gave birth to girl twins, Timolin and Casey. I was crazy about all my siblings, but the ironclad bond with Cooke was formed first. It was probably the most wonderful and satisfying relationship of my life.

1977

Our apartment was extremely modest. There was no money for fancy furniture, no frills of any kind. Yet I never felt deprived. Love lived in those tiny rooms where we lived—Mama's love.

I loved helping Mama in the kitchen. The pots were boiling, the tortillas sizzling in the skillet, and Mama was in a bubbly mood.

"Patricia," Mama said to me in Spanish, "I have something to tell you that will make you happy."

I couldn't imagine what it was.

"I'm going to have a baby."

"Will it be a girl?"

I had two younger brothers, whom I loved. But more than anything, I wanted a baby sister.

"If it is God's will," said Mama. "But boy or girl, a new baby is always a blessing. A new baby always brings joy."

Mama's pregnancy gave me joy. I was happy to help her in any way I could. Even though I was only ten, I was proficient at most of the household chores. I could cook and clean and do laundry. The more I did, the more useful I felt.

When it came time to go the hospital, I wanted to accompany my mother.

"Better that you care for your brothers."

The next day my mother's sister Esther—we called her Aunt Tete—called.

"You have a sister, *niña,*" she said.

I screamed with delight. "What's her name?"

"Jessica."

"Jessica's a beautiful name."

"Jessica's a beautiful baby."

"Can I come to the hospital to see her?"

"Not right away, sweetheart. The doctors have to give her some more medicine."

"I can help the doctors."

"I know you can, but just be a little patient and you'll see her soon."

I didn't see her soon.

We stayed in a Los Angeles neighborhood where other El Salvadoran families lived. With my mother still in the hospital, they, along with my own relatives, made sure that my brothers and I were okay. But I was uneasy. I wanted to see my mother, and of course my little sister, Jessica.

Then good news, again from Aunt Tete: Mama and Jessica were coming home. The night before, I was too excited to sleep. Next morning, I stood guard by the window and came running out the second the car pulled up to our apartment. There was Mama, but no Jessica.

Even as I was hugging my mother, I asked, "Where's my sister?"

"She can't come home yet, darling. She needs medicines and care that only the hospital can provide."

When I started crying, Mama took me in her arms.

"Will Jessica be okay?" I asked.

"If it's God's will, yes."

"And if it's not God's will?" I asked.

"The doctors are doing all they can."

"When can I see her?"

"You'll have to be patient, sweetheart."

I wasn't patient. I began composing letters to Jessica, welcoming her to the family. Each night I'd stare at the crib across from my bed, imagining what it would be like to have my infant sister sleep by my side.

It was not an easy time. Mama did not have a husband. Jessica's father was not the same man who had fathered me. Mama raised us alone, working three different jobs as a caretaker. She alone was burdened with the task of providing us with food and shelter.

For three long months she went to the hospital every day to see her newborn. When I kept asking what was wrong, I was told that Jessica was sick and required serious surgery. The words meant little to me. All I remember is being afraid that my sister was going to die—and I'd never get to see her.

Then one day I overheard Mama and Aunt Tete speaking in Spanish. I understood their every word: They had moved the baby from Martin Luther King Jr. Hospital, where she was born, to County Hospital, where the operation was performed. After the operation, a nurse wasn't careful with an IV tube and somehow infected Jessica. Knowing we were Catholic, the doctors suggested that Mama call a priest to baptize the baby.

I had to interrupt the conversation. It didn't matter that my mother would learn that I was eavesdropping.

"Why a priest?" I asked. "Is Jessica dying? I need to see her before she dies."

"She's sick," Aunt Tete explained, "but that doesn't mean she won't get better."

"Then why is she being baptized?"

"All babies born in our faith are baptized."

"Why can't we wait until she comes home and baptize her in a church? Isn't that how babies are usually baptized?"

"We're just being cautious, *niña,*" said Mama.

I knew that they were trying to keep me from being afraid, but I was afraid nonetheless. I prayed to God that my sister get well. Every night I looked at her crib and imagined her sleeping there. Every day when Mama left to see her at the hospital, I asked if I could come along. Every day I was told no; I was told to be patient. Every night when Mama returned, I asked about my sister.

At the end of the third month, I was looking out the window when I saw Aunt Tete's car drive up. I saw Mama was seated next to her. When Mama got out of the car, I saw she was holding a baby. I opened the door and ran like the wind to finally see my sister.

Her little eyes.

Her sweet little cheeks.

Her tiny fingers and fingernails.

A doll. My sister. My *hermanita.* A living doll. Alive and well.

"Can I hold her?" I asked Mama.

"Yes, just wait till we get inside, honey."

My brothers were curious to see her, but I was over the moon. I had to be the first one to put her in her crib.

"Handle her gently," said Mama.

I took my baby sister in my arms. She was light as a feather. I looked down at her eyes just as she was looking at me. I ever so gently laid her down in her crib. She closed her eyes and slept. I stood there the whole time, just watching.

I gave her a bottle that night. As she sucked in the milk, she kept looking at me.

"I'm Patty," I said. "I'm your big sister."

During the night, I woke up every twenty minutes or so to check on her. I wanted to make sure she was breathing. She was. She slept peacefully.

Jessica was finally home.

3

IT WAS STILL winter 2008 when I got Dr. Woolf to go along with my plan: I'd start treatments as soon as I completed my album. Cooke was urging me to go the natural route, but I was uncertain. All I knew was that I wanted to make music. Music has always made things better.

I know now that music, for all its healing properties, is also escape. I wanted to escape the reality of my medical condition by losing myself in music. As a kid, I wanted to escape the harsh emotional reality by doing the same. Whatever the problems with my mother, I always loved the fact that, like my dad, my mother was all about music. She had sung with Duke Ellington; her buddies were legendary divas like Lena Horne, Billie Holiday, and Dinah Washington. In our home, music was played night and day—Count Basie, Billy Eckstine, Peggy Lee, and June Christy. Like Dad, Mom had impeccable taste in music. No matter how great the tension in our home—and believe me, it *did* get tense—music was the one element that stayed steady, remained beautiful, and calmed the angry storms.

When it came to my music, Cooke had always been my biggest cheerleader.

"You're different than your colleagues, Sweetie," Cooke would say. "You're not just a singer. You're a musician."

When I was feeling down, or unsure, or pressured by the business, Cooke was always there with her wisdom.

"Music is your heart and your soul," she'd remind me. "Music is your way of expressing your love to the world. It's also your way of connecting to Dad."

Cooke was right, but Cooke was also modest. It was Cooke, in fact, who introduced me to the music that shaped my life. When we were kids I'd leave my bedroom, painted yellow, to go to Cooke's room, painted in a far cooler blue, to listen to what *she* was listening to. My room was filled with dolls and clowns and little books of verse. Cooke's room was filled with LPs like *Sing a Song of Basie* by Lambert, Hendricks & Ross, whose vocalese—putting words to instrumental solos—excited my imagination. Cooke was also excited by Broadway musicals. She directed me in putting on performances for our parents. We'd do "I'm Gonna Wash That Man Right Outa My Hair" from *South Pacific* or "Why Can't a Woman Be More Like a Man?" from *My Fair Lady*. In the early sixties, it was Cooke who hipped me to the Beatles, Cooke who appreciated rock and roll, even when our father was telling the world that "Mr. Cole won't rock and roll."

I remember Cooke winning over my father's heart when, for a class project, she concocted a mime version of jazz pianist Ahmad Jamal's "Poinciana." She dressed up in Dad's clothes—sports shirt, blazer, trousers, loafers, even his stingy-brim hat—and performed the song on a make-believe piano. I thought it was the coolest thing I'd ever seen. I thought Cooke was the coolest sister in the whole wide world.

Hep C or no hep C, I was going to lose myself in music. I was going to call Cooke every night for support. I was going to get through the winter and then worry about the treatments.

"How are you feeling, Sweetie?" Cooke called to ask.

"Feeling fine. I wouldn't know I had a rotten liver if the doctor hadn't told me."

"You taking those vitamins and minerals I gave you?"

"Every day."

"And meditating?"

As a Buddhist, Cooke was a firm believer in meditation. I have nothing against meditation, but sitting still just ain't my thing.

"I'm trying," I said.

"Did you decide to do another duet with Dad?"

"You like the idea of another duet?"

"Of course. The highlight of *Unforgettable* was you and Dad singing 'Unforgettable.' If this is in some way a follow-up record, you need to follow up with another duet."

"That's what I think. I'm doing 'Walkin' My Baby Back Home.' "

"Beautiful. Kelly always loved Dad's version."

The mention of Kelly always both gladdened and saddened my heart. We lost Kelly in 1995 to AIDS when he was only thirty-six. My brother was a beautiful man, physically and spiritually. He was only five when Dad died, and, as a result, grew up without a father. He grew up to love divas, not sports. He adored Sophie Tucker and Josephine Baker. He also became the family historian, dedicating himself to studying and collecting every recording my father ever made.

Kelly came out of the closet to me in 1976 when he was seventeen. He knew I wouldn't judge him, and I didn't. Because he read everything about the Coles, he had seen an article in *Ebony* that Dad had written called "Why We

Adopted Kelly." In it, our father had mentioned that he wanted a son who loved sports and would be a good athlete. That simply wasn't Kelly.

"Would he have been disappointed in me?" Kelly asked when he revealed his homosexuality.

"Dad was from another time and place," I said.

"He wouldn't have approved, would he?"

"He'd have come to love you the way we've all come to love you," I insisted. "Dad had some old-fashioned attitudes—we all do—but that doesn't mean he wouldn't have been proud to have a son as bright and beautiful as you."

"You don't think he would have disowned me?"

"Please. Dad? Look at the prejudice he encountered. You know better than me what he went through. Some man attacked him while he was onstage in Alabama just because he was black. They wouldn't air his TV show in the South because they didn't want a handsome dark-skinned black man singing love songs to an audience of white women. Dad might have had prejudices of his own, but they weren't deep-rooted. He was the victim of hatred himself, and I know damn well that would have kept him from victimizing anyone else—especially his own son."

Kelly appreciated the support and knew, through both Cooke and me, that his father's love was real.

Kelly and I didn't always see eye-to-eye. As he grew older and fell into a promiscuous lifestyle that I considered dangerous, I let him know that I didn't approve. For several years, we were estranged. But when the virus hit, Kelly stayed with me for a little while. He spoke about his treatment and, for the first time, I heard the word *interferon.*

There were religious differences among us. For most of Kelly's life, he considered himself an agnostic. I'd always considered myself a Christian, and in the seventies, I was baptized as a Baptist—as was my son. Kelly, Cooke, and I would have animated and sometimes heated conversations: Kelly, who didn't know what to believe, Cooke chanting and lighting incense all over the place, and me walking around with my Bible. We were quite a sight.

I was astonished and grateful when, during his battle with AIDS, Kelly told me he was attending St. Victor's, a gay-friendly church in Los Angeles. He also said that he had accepted Christ. I considered that a miracle. In Kelly's last days, he had a calmness of spirit that can only come with the knowledge that you are loved by a supernatural force. Kelly will never be forgotten. We love him now, and we always will.

4

MEANWHILE, I HAD a record to make.

"What other songs are you including?" Cooke asked.

"Remember a couple of years back I was at the Grammys and Tony Bennett told me about a tune called 'Coffee Time.' "

"You were going to try to find it."

"Well, I did. It was sung in 1960 in a movie called *The Subterraneans.* And guess who sang it?"

"I know Jack Kerouac wrote the novel."

"Well, Carmen McRae sang the song."

"Mom was friends with Carmen."

"I know. Wait till you hear it, Cooke! Reminds me of when you and I used to spend our evenings drinking coffee, smoking cigarettes, and talking much shit."

Cooke laughed.

"Send me the rough demo, Sweetie. I know you'll kill it."

Being in the studio allowed me to avoid obsessing over the medical treatments that awaited me. I wasn't hiding from reality as much as entering into another reality—the reality of music. Nothing triggers nostalgia like music. Songs are tied to memories. Memories bring us back to moments in our life, painful or joyful, that demand reflection. When I sing, I remember.

When I worked at Capitol Studios in the famous Hollywood tower designed to resemble a stack of records—some called it the tower that Nat built—I inevitably thought of my father. He recorded for the Capitol label and did many of his recordings in the very studio where, on the wall, there's a photo of him with Louis Armstrong and Ella Fitzgerald. Seven-year-old Natalie is standing by her daddy's side. How could this studio not provide an ambience of nourishment, warmth, and love?

One of the songs I decided to sing was a Jack Jones hit from the early sixties, "Lollipops and Roses." I loved it the first time I heard it and presumed it was about little girls.

Later I understood its message to mean that men must cater to women. Whatever its adult connotations, the song retained a sweetness I found irresistible.

Recording at Capitol also had me remembering the time Dad took me to boarding school in Massachusetts. It happened in 1964, a couple of years after "Lollipops" came out. We made the trip alone, without Mom, and I cherished our time together. Northfield School for Girls was an exclusive academy attended predominantly by children of wealthy whites. I don't think Dad expected the greeting he received: Walking through campus, he was mobbed; everyone wanted an autograph or a handshake. He was applauded as though he were onstage.

"Now, you be good, Sweetie," he said after dropping me off at the dorm. "Christmas will be here before you know it, and we'll all be together again."

I hated the thought of his leaving. That night I cried myself to sleep. I missed Dad already. I'd never known anyone so comfortable in his own skin. My father was Mr. Kick-Back-and-Relax, Mr. Take-It-as-It-Comes, Mr. Go-with-the-Flow. When Dad was home in his easy chair, he loved watching roller derby and baseball. I'd sit next to him. Come the seventh-inning stretch, we'd steal away to the kitchen for sardine sandwiches.

I remembered the day Mom gave him a sports car for his birthday.

"Sweetie," said Dad, "you and I are going riding in style."

Other than Dad, I was the only one in the family who loved speed. I loved that slate-gray Jaguar with its flaming-red interior and coal-black convertible top. I loved slipping in the seat beside him and zipping through the streets of Hollywood, Dad devil-driving like Steve McQueen.

I thought about that the night he left me at Northfield. Dad was always leaving. I was always comforted, though, by the certain fact that he'd be back. And when he returned, the world was right again.

After he dropped me off at school, I enjoyed some status as "the daughter of." But that feeling didn't last long. It was my first separation from Cooke, and I missed her terribly. Most of the girls were from "old money"—and by old, I mean New England families from Revolutionary days. There was a prejudice against the nouveau riche. The academic demands were intense and the teachers cold. I wasn't happy.

So it was with great anticipation that I looked forward to Christmas. Dad didn't play his records at home, except for the holidays. "The Christmas Song"—"Chestnuts roasting on an open fire"—was on heavy rotation. Our tree was magnificent, and friends and family stopped by every day with gifts and good cheer.

When I arrived home, I couldn't wait to see Dad.

"Don't bother him now, Sweetie," said Mom. "He's under the weather."

She spoke the words strangely. I knew something was wrong.

I waited all afternoon. Dad didn't come down for supper, and afterward I asked Mom if he was feeling better.

"He's just tired, Sweetie."

The next day, unable to wait any longer, I went to his bedroom and knocked on the door. In a voice that barely sounded like his, he told me to come in.

I was shocked when I saw him sitting in his rocking chair. He looked like a ghost. I wanted to cry but held back the tears. I ran over and kissed him. He managed a smile and touched my cheek. He appeared to be twice his age. His hair had turned white; his body was skeletal, his eyes hollow, his skin ashen.

Mom hadn't told us, hadn't prepared us, hadn't been able to deal with it herself. When I questioned her about Dad's horrible condition, her answers were evasive. "He's being treated by the best doctors in the city . . . it isn't anything to worry about . . . your father will be fine."

I desperately wanted to believe those words, but I couldn't. I knew Dad was dying.

After I went back to school in January, my mother sent me a telegram that Dad's left lung had been removed and the operation was a success. Then, in the middle of February, I was in biology lab, thinking how much I disliked the smell of formaldehyde, when I was told to report to my dorm. My housemother didn't have to say a word. Her eyes told me. Dad was gone. He died on February 15, 1965.

I didn't cry. I went numb. I simply packed and headed for the airport. Cooke picked me up and drove me home. Mom, dressed in black, met us at the front door. I had never seen her in black before. She was a woman who loved high fashion and vivid colors. Seeing her black dress did something to me. The floodgates erupted; I broke down and wept like a baby. Cooke held me in her arms.

Cooke took me to the Angelus Funeral Home to view Dad's body. It was just the two of us in a room with his open coffin. We couldn't look at him for long. Seeing his lifeless body was so traumatic, we had to sit down to keep from fainting.

Our dad had a strange habit: When you were telling him a story about what happened during your day, he didn't respond immediately. He might be busy reading a newspaper or watching a ball game. Then, minutes after, he'd turn and say, "Huh?" He did this often and it used to drive me and Cooke nuts.

Well, when Cooke and I were sitting at the funeral home in front of my father's casket, trying to process the terrible pain of losing him, the room was perfectly quiet. After a few minutes, we heard a voice say, "Huh?"

Cooke looked at me and I looked at her.

"Did you hear what I heard?" asked Cooke.

"What'd you hear?"

" 'Huh?' "

"You heard 'huh?' " I asked.

"I heard 'huh?' What'd you hear?"

" 'Huh?' "

And then, without thinking twice, we ran like hell.

Once outside, I said, "It was Dad, wasn't it, Cooke?"

"It was his voice," my sister confirmed.

"How could it have been?"

"You tell me. Are you sure?"

"I am. I heard it clear as day."

"I did, too."

Forty-five years have passed since I heard that voice, and I still swear it was Dad. In that period of despair, Dad gave us a moment of grace—and you'll never convince me otherwise!

During the period that followed Dad's death, his voice was everywhere. His songs were played nonstop. The funeral, at St. James' Episcopal Church in L.A., was massive. Stars, politicians, and everyday people came out to tell him good-bye. My mother reminded me of Jackie Kennedy. She was perfectly poised, maintaining great dignity amid this profound sadness. We were required to act the same.

Days passed and it was time to return to Northfield. I begged Mom to let me stay home and transfer to high school in L.A. But she insisted that I go back; she said she would be fine. I now see that she was unable to comfort me because she was unable to comfort herself. As a sixty-year-old woman, I understand. As a fifteen-year-old girl, I didn't.

I went back to boarding school but eventually did return to L.A., where I graduated from a private high school in the Valley. I felt the absence of my father every single day. It was the first loss in my life, and its impact was beyond my comprehension.

I graduated from high school, and in 1972, I graduated from the University of Massachusetts with a major in psychology. In the meantime, though, I had started going crazy—emotionally, physically, even sexually. Mix that in with the turbulent times—the Vietnam War, the protest movement, a culture high on drugs.

I totally rebelled against my mother. I stole, I drank, I discovered drugs. I discovered a black identity and separated myself from upper-class society. I became a Black Panther advocate and had the Afro and the dashiki—oh yes, all of that. And somehow, in the midst of that, I discovered that I could sing a little. I loved jazz and rock and R & B; I loved all kinds of music and yet I was adamant on a single point: I absolutely refused to sing any songs even remotely associated with my father.

"She's Not a Doll, She's a Real Person."

My preteen years were all about Jessica.

"Patty," Mama would tell me, "babies can easily hurt themselves. You have to watch them at all times."

"I understand."

"An accident can happen in less than a second. Babies are fragile."

"I'd never let anything happen to Jessica," I said.

"Never on purpose, I know. But it's easy to get distracted. Don't forget that when I'm not here, Jessica is your responsibility."

"Don't worry, Mama. I'll keep my eye on her."

"And your arms and hands as well."

"Of course. She's my *hermanita*, my little doll."

"She's not a doll, Patty. She's a real person, and real people have real injuries."

I knew Mama didn't want to leave Jessica, but when Mama worked on the weekends or late at night, she had no choice. I wanted to earn her trust. There's nothing I wanted to do more than take good care of Jessica.

"Now you sit here in your high chair," I told Jessica after Mama had left for work. "I'll fix your food and you'll eat while I do the chores."

Even when she was barely two years old, I talked to Jessica

as if she could understand me. Her expression had me believing that my words made sense. "Yes," she seemed to be saying, "you clean and I'll eat."

I placed her in the high chair and brought her food, Gerber's mashed-up sweet potatoes. I spoon-fed her until she lost interest.

"Okay," I said, "I'll be right back to feed you the rest. I just have a little cleaning to do."

A little cleaning turned out to be a lot of cleaning. When I get started, it's hard to stop. I do a job till it's done. On that day, the job was mopping the kitchen floor, vacuuming the rugs, and cleaning the bathroom from top to bottom. When Mama got home, I wanted her to see that our place was sparkling. I kept scrubbing, scrubbing, scrubbing. I was on my knees wiping down the bathtub when suddenly I realized I'd forgotten about Jessica! I hadn't heard a sound from her in over a half hour!

I ran to the kitchen, where—oh, my God!—she had fallen face-first into her food. Petrified, I picked up her face and made sure she was breathing. She was. Her eyes, nose, mouth, and cheeks were covered with sweet potato. She was a mess—and fast asleep.

I picked her up out of the chair, carried her to the bathroom, and gave her a quick bath, careful not to make the water too hot. I could tell that she loved the way the water felt on her skin. I dried her off, diapered her, and dressed her in her pink bunny pajamas. When I put her down in her crib, I said, "Jessica, you don't have to tell Mama what happened tonight, do you?"

When she looked up, I heard her heart say, "You're my big sister, Patty, and your secret is safe with me."

5

I'D BEEN TOLD about my hep C condition in the winter of 2008.

By spring, I had still not started treatments. All my concentration was on music. I played dates on the road, and as soon as I got back to L.A., I ran to the studio and kept working on *Still Unforgettable.*

"How's the record progressing?" asked Cooke during one of our late-night calls that I had come to cherish and value so much throughout the years—and tears.

"Tomorrow I'm recording 'You Go to My Head.' "

"Love that song. Who suggested it?"

"Dick."

"Dick knows every cool song ever written."

Dick LaPalm is a dear friend of our family and a beautiful man I've known all my life. He's a formidable scholar of pop music and jazz, a former record executive, and a treasured consultant to me. Dick helped me pick all the songs for *Unforgettable . . . with Love* and contributed greatly to *Still Unforgettable.* As far as Dick is concerned, though, his real claim to fame is being Dad's best friend.

"I was thinking about Dad the other night," said Cooke. "Remember the night we went to see him at the Hollywood Bowl?"

"Are you kidding? I'll never forget it!"

The memory came flooding back.

"How old was I?" I asked Cooke.

"Probably around eight."

"So you were thirteen. Remember going backstage before the show began?"

"Of course."

"Dad was sitting there in his silk robe. He had his cigarette holder . . ."

"He always had his cigarette holder."

"And a do-rag on his head."

"In those days," said Cooke, "all the cats processed their hair."

"I remember looking at him to see if he was nervous."

"Dad? Never."

"Right. Cool as a cucumber. There he was, about to play

in front of seventeen thousand fans, and you'd think he'd be a little anxious. But he wasn't even fazed."

"They asked us if we wanted to watch the show from the wings."

"And I said no. I wanted to see him the way the audience saw him. So Sparky—remember Sparky?"

"Sure," said Cooke. "Dad's right-hand man."

"Sparky took us to our seats in the front row."

"And you freaked out, Sweetie."

"Oh God, you're right. I freaked because there was a reflecting pool in front of the stage—"

"And you were convinced Dad was going to fall into it!"

"I thought he'd drown."

"I kept telling you that it wasn't going to happen."

"And I kept seeing it happen."

"Talking about the Hollywood Bowl, was it at the Bowl or the Greek that you saw Sinatra and Sarah Vaughan?"

"The Greek. Which reminds me—I'm doing 'Nice 'n' Easy' on *Still Unforgettable*."

"That's Sinatra's song. Dad never sang it."

"This record is more than a tribute to Dad," I explained. "It's a tribute to all the icons of the day."

"Well, 'Nice 'n' Easy' is a good emotional mantra for you, Sweetie. It's the way you're going to get through your little health thing."

"I'm still not thinking about my little health thing. Don't want to think about it until this record is finished. Right now, I'm thinking about Sinatra. I'm going to sing 'Here's That Rainy Day' because Sinatra was the first one I heard sing it."

"That same night at the Greek?"

"Yes. That's also the night I first met Sarah. It was Sarah who introduced me to Drue, my son's nanny."

"Beautiful Drue," said Cooke. "May she rest in peace."

My mind raced back to that night at the Greek. It was 1977. I attended the concert with Marvin Yancy, my then husband. I was pregnant with our son, Robbie.

As always, Sinatra was superb. His rendering of "Rainy Day" had me mesmerized. When Sarah sang "Send In the Clowns," they practically had to send for smelling salts to revive me.

After the show, I went to see Frank, who'd been friends with my father and was always encouraging.

"I love those songs of yours they're playing on the radio, Sweetie," he said. "I can imagine how proud your dad would be."

When I visited Sarah backstage, she was also supportive. "How old are you, Natalie?" she asked.

"Twenty-seven."

"And how many hits have you had?"

"A few."

"More than a few. Anyway, baby, when I was twenty-seven I had exactly no hits."

"What about 'Broken Hearted Melody'?" I asked. "That was a big hit."

"Didn't hit till I was well into my thirties, and I didn't even like the damn song!"

I told Sassy that certain singers are bigger than hits; some singers are forever—like Sarah Vaughan.

When we got through chatting, Sarah introduced me to Drue, who happened to be the sister of the woman who had cooked for me. Drue worked as a nanny for Sarah's daughter, Paris.

"Paris is too old for a nanny now, but it seems like you may be needing one soon," said Sarah, pointing to my stomach. "Drue is the absolute best."

Sarah was right. A few days later, I interviewed Drue and hired her on the spot. Drue McCrae became a cornerstone in the life of my family and a second mom to my son, Rob.

Eight years later—eight years of being Rob's second mom—Drue died tragically, just two years after the death of Rob's father, Marvin, the love of my life.

Death piled upon death. Too young, too soon, too suddenly.

Which brought me back to the first and worst death I had encountered—the death of my dad.

Here, though, in the studio, my dad lived.

I brought him to life.

He brought me to life.

I was his baby, and he was walking his baby back home.

In the studio, death had no dominion.

In the studio, there was only music, eternal hope, and memory-soaked melodies. For example, Cooke and I singing "We Are Siamese" from *Lady and the Tramp* while my parents applauded their adorable daughters.

Now I was a grown lady recording "Until the Real Thing Comes Along," as I remembered being thirteen-year-old Natalie listening to Aretha Franklin sing the same song on an album called *Laughing on the Outside*, the same Aretha who also sang a song sung by Nat Cole, "But Beautiful," on her record *Soft and Beautiful.*

Beautiful father, beautiful Aretha, beautiful songs—all *Still Unforgettable.*

As I sang "But Beautiful," I thought of the beautiful musical influences that shaped my soul and I gave thanks to God.

After a magical night in the studio, I came home to unwind and noticed a message on the machine.

"Miss Cole," said the voice, "this is Dr. Woolf's nurse. He'd like to know when you can begin your treatments."

I erased the message and went to bed, my mind lulled by the music.

• • •

A week passed.

"Almost done?" asked Cooke during our nightly call.

"Almost."

"What are you working on now?"

" 'Something's Gotta Give.' "

"I bet you're thinking about how Sammy sang it, right, Sweetie?"

"You know me too well."

Sammy Davis Jr. was our Uncle Sammy; his wife, our Aunt Altovise. When I started my career, Sammy was among the first to reach out and assure me that I'd make it. He was all positive energy. Toward the end of his life, though, when he invited me to Vegas to see his show, I was heartbroken. Cancer was killing him. On his face I saw the same ashen pallor that I had seen on my father's face when I came home that fateful Christmas.

When I sang "Something's Gotta Give," though, I didn't think about the sick Sammy, but the always-energetic, brilliantly talented Sammy. I loved recording this album. I didn't want the recording process to end.

"You're a Good Mama"

I don't remember her exact age, but I do remember the exact moment.

I was pushing Jessica in her stroller down to a park in Santa Monica near our apartment. It was a sunny day, and I could feel a breeze from the ocean only a few blocks away. There was a birthday party. Balloons were strung from the trees and children were running around us in every direction. Jessica couldn't have been happier. She had started to make little noises but hadn't said a real word. I'd been trying to get her to say my name for weeks.

"Patty," I said to her slowly. "Say Patty."

She'd just smile and make a nonsense sound.

"Patty," I repeated. "Listen to me, *hermanita*. I'm your sister, Patty."

It was important for me to hear her say my name.

I could see that she wanted to get out of her stroller, so I picked her up and put her on the grass. She crawled around, happy as she could be. One of the kids from the party came over and gave her a balloon. Jessica squealed with delight. She soon got bored with the balloon and spotted a little puppy that she wanted to touch. I asked the owner, a young woman, if that was okay. She said yes, and the dog licked Jessica's face. She liked it and started laughing.

Then she looked up at me and said the word, clear as day.

"Mama."

"I'm Patty," I said. "I'm not your mama. Mama's working today."

"Mama," she repeated, looking right into my eyes.

"Patty," I repeated, trying to correct her.

But she wouldn't have it. I was Mama.

When it was time to go home, I picked her up from the grass and held her upright. I had a feeling something special was about to happen, so, as she stood there, I removed my hands from her sides. That's when she took her first two steps before plopping back down.

"You're a good mama," the puppy's owner said to me. "You're teaching your baby how to walk."

6

May 2008

Me and Cooke, blabbering on the phone.

"It's all beautiful music. It's all tied to Dad and the singers of his generation," Cooke said after hearing a rough mix of *Still Unforgettable*. "Your voice sounds great. You sound like you've forgotten about whatever little health challenges you might be facing."

"I did forget about them," I said. "On purpose."

"And now purposefully you must face them."

"Right now it just pretty much sucks. Doesn't Mr. Hepatitis know I have work to do?"

"You'll do it. But I hope without the chemo."

"You can be sure that I'll let you know."

"Don't stress, Sweetie. However you wanna do it, I'm with you."

"Your words mean the world to me, Cooke. You know how much I love you."

"Love you, too, sis."

Still Unforgettable was complete. I had done all the sweetening and tweaking required. I liked the way my co-producer, Gail Deadrick, and I had shaped the record. It was a good solid piece of music, but I still was not able to let it go. So I recorded five "bonus tracks," including a song I had long loved, "How Do You Keep the Music Playing?" That was the question I was asking myself. The answer, of course, was to keep singing. Medical treatments or not, I wasn't about to abandon my music.

When I look back at this, I see that I was most certainly entering into the River of De Nile!

Anything to keep me from having to face chemo. And yet, despite my sister's objections, chemo is ultimately what I chose. Before that, though, Cooke had introduced me to her good friend who started me on a serious homeopathic treatment of energy drinks, protein drinks, wheatgrass, and packets of every imaginable vitamin. The hope was that this alternative method might strengthen and heal my liver. But the problem was that my liver was in an advanced stage of deterioration. If I was going to keep it, I needed a strong jolt of medicine.

So I went with the chemo treatment. I saw it as my best chance for survival. And interferon, a potent antiviral medicine, was deemed the most effective treatment.

When I finally made the appointment with Dr. Woolf to tell him my decision, I asked my friends Benita and Tammy to accompany me. I needed moral support.

"I'm ready," I told Dr. Woolf. "How does it work?"

"You inject yourself once a week."

"Yuck. Where?" I asked.

"Your thigh. One week your left thigh, next week the right, and so on. This is similar to what a diabetic does with insulin."

"What about the side effects?"

"You'll have flulike symptoms. A low fever, low energy. You probably won't feel like eating much."

"And how long will this go on?" I asked.

"At least six months."

"Will I last that long?"

"Of course."

Dr. Woolf then showed me how to stick myself.

Who knew that a tiny little needle could bring a grown man or, in this case, a grown woman to her knees? No one can prepare you for the physical and emotional toll this stuff puts on you.

The doctor called them flulike symptoms. I'd call them deathlike symptoms.

After the first injections, I was a total mess. I remembered Kelly's reaction to interferon when he was battling AIDS. Now I found myself experiencing the same things: no appetite, vomiting for days, painfully aching joints, alarming weight loss, no energy, so tired I couldn't come off the pillow.

I felt like the world was falling down around me, and the first person I called was Cooke.

"Cooke," I said, "I feel like death warmed over."

I knew Cooke would never say "I told you so" concerning the chemotherapy—she was far too compassionate to throw that in my face—but I knew what she was thinking.

"You'll get through this, Sweetie," she said. "You've got the heart of a lioness."

"And the body of a skeleton. Know how much weight I've lost these first two weeks?"

"You haven't been eating, so of course you're losing weight."

"Twenty goddamn pounds, Cooke! Twenty pounds in two weeks!"

"You'll put it back on."

"I was in better shape strung out on heroin."

"Let's not romanticize your heroin days. I was there, remember?"

My mind flashed back to New York in the seventies. I lived to get high. I lived to stay high. The fact that my first album hit big didn't compare to the high I felt when I hit the needle. And despite the good money I was making, I always needed more money for drugs.

At the time, Cooke was living the bohemian life in a loft in SoHo and enjoying a promising acting career. Cicely Tyson and Ruby Dee were singing her praises. She was doing film as well as theater. She was featured in the original *Taking of Pelham One Two Three* with Walter Matthau. She was also sympathetic to my plight. Once or twice Cooke and I had gotten high together—on weed. She understood the get-high life.

"But you abuse that life," she said when I came running to her place in New York, using it as a pit stop for my drug runs. "You'll never be able to do drugs moderately, Sweetie. You've got an addictive personality. With you, it's all or nothing. You've got to get off the stuff."

"I will. I plan to."

"When?"

"Later. Right now I need to keep from getting sick."

"So you're saying the money you want from me is for your health."

"In a manner of speaking . . ."

"In a manner of speaking, Sweetie, you're full of shit."

"I just need—"

"What you need is to hit bottom. And staying here isn't helping you any. Any comfort I give you isn't comfort at all. It's actually harm. Much as it pains me, I gotta stop harming you. I can't give you any money and I can't let you stay here any longer."

"Is this what they call tough love?" I asked.

"Doesn't matter what it's called, it's how I feel. I love you too much to help you destroy yourself."

I understood. I left. Later I saw the deep wisdom of Cooke's ways. I needed to crash before I found my way to rehab. I needed to hear myself make those ridiculous promises to God—"Please let me score this one last time and I swear never to do it again"—only to do it again and again until even I couldn't live with my lies.

Now a lifetime later Cooke was telling me, "The state of your soul is strong, sis. You're going to make it."

It was a brutal period.

Shortly after my hep C diagnosis, I issued a press release with a truthful account of my condition. I did it as both a warning to drug abusers and a way to dispel untrue rumors. But as my appearance continued to deteriorate, rumors flew nonetheless. I was said to have every disease from AIDS to early Alzheimer's.

I looked at the calendar. It was June 2008, and I had ten days of dates in Tokyo. By then, I was on oxygen and too weak to walk any distances. I was wheeled through airports.

"You gotta cancel Japan," Cooke said. "It's too much."

"My most loyal fans are in Japan," I replied. "They're counting on me."

"They'll wait."

"The shows are sold out."

"Ever hear of refunds?"

"I can't disappoint them."

"You can't do this to yourself, Sweetie."

"I'll call you when I get there, Cooke."

The flight over was hell. I couldn't keep anything down. Soon as I got to the hotel in Tokyo, I called my sister.

"I made it."

"You sound terrible."

"I'll be better when I start singing."

"For God's sake, Sweetie, take it easy, and call me after your first show."

I went to the club. An IV had been set up in my dressing room. All I could eat was a few bites of steamed rice.

After the show, I called Cooke.

"How'd it go?" she asked.

"When they wheeled me out onstage and the audience got their first look at me, I heard this loud gasp. They thought they were looking at a corpse."

"Well, could the corpse sing?"

"That's the funny part, Cooke. The voice was there. I sang well. The response was tremendous. I saw some people crying. Maybe they thought this was the last time they'd ever see me alive."

"Oh, you'll be back. Long as you don't stay too long. Try and come home early."

"I don't think that's going to happen."

It didn't. I put my head down and somehow managed to get through all the dates. At the Blue Note, the most prestigious jazz club in Japan, you play two shows a night. By the end of the last show on the last night, I was toast.

The minute the plane from Tokyo landed in L.A., I rushed straight to Dr. Woolf, who had been concerned about whether I could tolerate the trip.

I was in the examining room with him for no more than five minutes before I began throwing up. If it hadn't been so pitiful, it would have been funny, watching the good doctor running around the room, looking for something—a bowl, a container, *anything*—for me to use.

"It can't get any worse than this, can it?" I asked him.

When he didn't answer, I knew I was in trouble.

Growing Up Fast

Jessica was an easy baby who grew into a sweet little girl. Like me, she had to grow up fast. Because Mama was at work, we learned to be self-sufficient. By the time Jessica was ten—my age when she was born—she could do all the household chores.

My main memory of Jessica as a child is her generosity. She loved to give. Fact is, giving was her nature. If Mama came home with a present for her—say, a doll—the first thing she'd do is share it with a friend. And if Jessica's friend didn't have a doll of her own, Jessica would say, "Here, keep mine." Most kids are possessive, but Mama would actually have to lecture Jessica about not giving everything away. At other kids' birthday parties, Jessica always helped the mother serve the cake. Everyone had to have their slice before Jessica sat down to eat hers.

When she was eleven and I was twenty-one, I married Arturo, the love of my life, and left home. I know Jessica would have liked me to stay with her and Mama through the rest of her childhood, but that wasn't possible. I told her I'd come by as often as possible, and I did. We continued to be close. But because I began working at White Memorial Hospital in Boyle Heights, far from where Jessica lived with Mama, I couldn't see her as often as I would have liked. Consequently, Jessica was alone a great deal of the time. But that didn't seem to affect her carefree spirit.

As a teen, she had lots of friends, including boys. To help out our mother, she worked at McDonald's and, after high school, took business courses. When she was eighteen, she met Solomon, her first serious relationship. Soon they married, and when Jessica was nineteen, she called and said, "Patty, how do you feel about becoming an aunt?"

"How do you feel about becoming a mother, *hermanita*?"

"I couldn't be happier."

"Then I'm happy as well."

"Will you tell Mama for me?"

"Why can't you tell Mama yourself?"

"She might get mad. She'll say I'm too young to have a baby. She'll say Solomon and I don't have enough money to support a child."

"No, Jessica. Mama will rejoice."

"Are you sure?"

"Positive. The news might shock her a little at first. But she'll come around. She'll celebrate with the rest of us."

When Richard was born, we were all thrilled. As a new mother, Jessica positively glowed. Her maternal instincts blossomed. I had been mothered with great gentleness and affection; I had tried to mother Jessica in a similar way; and now Jessica was demonstrating all those qualities in mothering Richard.

Life was good.

7

THEY SAY FAKE it till you make it, but I wasn't making it and I had reached the point where I could no longer fake it. Neither could the man, by the way, whom I had been dating. To save him any embarrassment, I'll call him Mr. Soave Bolla. Before my hep C kicked in, Mr. Bolla had expressed strong romantic interest in me. A man of considerable culture and charm, he seemed to enjoy taking me to fine restaurants and chic clubs. I liked his style. I thought he had a subtle mind and positive outlook on life. When sickness changed my life, he said, "Natalie, I'm here for you." That lasted a good month. Little by little, I saw him less and less. His calls of concern became less frequent. He suddenly had a number of trips that took him out of town for long periods. Finally, Mr. Bolla bounced.

I understood. The man wanted a healthy woman, not a scarecrow. I would have been more comfortable, though, had he been straight-up and said, "Look, Natalie, you're sick, and I'm having a hard time dealing with that. I'm not up to the task." I respect that kind of man. We all have our limitations. But Mr. Bolla didn't have the balls for that. He crawled away, like a snake.

Good-bye to old heartaches.

Hello to new agony.

There was no time to cry over jive-talking men. In September I had to go to New York, where I had a demanding schedule of media appearances to promote *Still Unforgettable.*

"I'm not sure you should make this trip," said Cooke the day before I left.

"It's important, sis. I worked too hard on this record not to promote it."

"Postpone it for a couple of months."

"By then I'll lose the momentum."

"Better than losing your sanity, Sweetie."

"I lost that a long time ago." I laughed.

"So I can't talk you into staying here and resting awhile?"

With Dad, Nat "King" Cole. I'm the little one, in an outfit identical to Cooke's—just the cutest!

In the backyard of our Hancock Park estate:
Cooke holding Princess, Mom, Dad, Mr. Pep, and me.

My brother, Kelly—beautiful, smart, and a very funny guy. We miss him terribly.

Cooke with John, her precious partner of thirty-plus years.

Cooke reunited with her beloved daughter, Caroline.

At the Grammy Awards on Unforgettable night in 1992:
me, Aunt Bay, and my dear friend Cecille.

Out on the town with my best escort—my son, Robbie!

A family photo: me, my sister Casey, Robbie, and my sister Timolin, at the top of the Capitol Records Tower in Los Angeles.

With my nephew Harleigh (left) and my son, Robbie, percussionists at a recording session in L.A. Aren't they cutie-pies?

With Denise Rich on New Year's Eve, 2006. I was the picture of health. If only I knew . . .

The women who arranged for the transplant that saved my life: Patty Argueta and her blessed mother, Dina Vasquez.

My donor family at OneLegacy. From the left: my cousin Pamela Harris, Arturo and Patty Argueta, me, Nurse Esther, Dina Vasquez, my close friend Tammy Engelstein, and Patty and Jessica's aunt Belinda.

The connection: Patty reaching out to Jessica.

Beautiful Jessica Karina, my donor.

My longtime friend of more than thirty years, Benita Hill Johnson, who helped me weather the storm.

Backstage at the Hollywood Bowl after my first big concert following the surgery. From the left: Barbara Rose, my manager; friend Tammy Engelstein; and my girl Friday, Pamela Harris.

"I'll rest in between appearances in New York."

"No one rests in New York."

"I promise to take a hot bath every night. I'll call you when I'm in the tub and you can remind me to slow down."

"Only Aunt Bay could slow you down. I wish she were here. She'd get you off this crazy schedule."

On the plane to New York, I thought of Bay. She was my bridge over troubled water. Back in the seventies, when I was busted in Canada for holding heroin, I couldn't return to the States for months. When the case was finally resolved, I ran to Chicago and the tiny little apartment where Aunt Bay and her daughter Janice lived.

Evelyn Coles—Coles was the original family name before Dad cut off the *s*—was my father's sister. We called her Bay. She had a hair salon and lived in the projects. She never left her roots or her Jesus. Jesus was her all. She was a praying woman, a fierce Christian who, no matter how badly I was behaving, never gave up on me—not for a second.

As a twentysomething, even as my musical talent blossomed, I continued to rage against the system. Dad was gone and Mom was busy raising my twin sisters and brother. I needed something but didn't know what. Bay knew. Bay knew I needed God.

I found God in Bay's apartment—in the praying hands sculpture that sat on her bedroom dresser and the plastic plaque on the living room windowsill that said "Expect a Miracle." Aunt Bay was my miracle. Every night I shared her bed. I felt like a girl in need of a mom. Bay became that mom. She took me to the Third Baptist Church, where I was baptized and washed clean in the blood of a loving savior. She changed my outlook and rearranged my heart. Her daughter Janice began coming to my gigs and became my spiritual advisor. Now there was praying before every show; there was gratitude; the greatness of a living God was acknowledged.

Bay acknowledged her blessings even when none seemed apparent. If the refrigerator was empty, Bay didn't worry; she simply prayed. A day later, you couldn't close the door for all the food stuffed inside. The woman had a direct line to God.

"Grace," Bay would say, "isn't about anything you do. It isn't about anything you earn. It's not based on you, Sweetie. It's based on Him, His nature, His forgiving ways. He can't do anything *but* love you because He is love. It's good to read the Bible and go to church. I love going to church. But if I never stepped in a church again, the Lord would love me just as much as if I had built Him a church taller than the Sears Tower. All we got to do is let ourselves feel that love. When we do, we're changed in every way. When we do, we're born again."

I was born again, but I fell again. Temptation got me. Bad choices got me. Drugs pulled me back, or rather, I let them pull me back. In 1981, I was on the twenty-fourth floor on the Vegas Hilton, on my hands and knees, about to take a hit off the crack pipe while the hotel was engulfed in fire. The door blew open, two firemen led me, my cousin Janice, and my bodyguard to safety, but for the next two years I was still fooling with Quaaludes and beer, smashing up my car, abusing my body, and neglecting my responsibilities until I had to leave Robbie with his nanny, Drue, and go off to Hazelden and the land of rehab.

You can say I was born again in rehab. It was 1983 and I was thirty-three. I saw that the Twelve Steps are steps toward surrendering to the God I had seen in Bay. I saw the mantra of "one day at a time" as a reminder that an ever-present, ever-loving God is eternal time. Stay with God and you stay in the present. Go to the past and regurgitate regret. Jump to the future and surround yourself with fear. God is neither behind you nor ahead of you. God is always right here, right now. God will get you through.

God got me through rehab. He was in every one of the steps. I had mismanaged my finances and messed up my career, but after recovery, I was working my way toward reconciliation with my husband, Marvin, the man who was, in part, responsible for my career.

Marvin and his partner Chuck Jackson produced my first album that contained my first hits. Those were songs written with my idol, Aretha Franklin, in mind. When Aretha decided not to sing them, I was lucky enough to be in the right place at the right time. After many months, with the record complete, Marvin asked me out on a date.

"Let's go to church," he said.

As a new Christian, I was only too happy to say yes. As a woman, I had been drawn to Marvin since the day we met. His musical gifts were extraordinary. Even more, he was a man of intellect and compassion. He was all about love.

At church, he sat me on the first pew and said he'd be right back. When he returned, he was walking down the aisle in a preacher's robe. Turned out that this was *his* church. All this time and Marvin never told me that he was a minister of God.

"God is bringing you two together," said Aunt Bay. "It's a providential arrangement."

I did a fine job of screwing up the arrangement. I drew Marvin into my world of drugs. Flying high on heroin, I had no idea how to nurture and preserve a marriage. We lasted less than four years. Thanks to my instability, I was making one bad decision after another. My worst decision was filing for divorce.

I was awarded custody of our son, Robbie, whom Marvin visited often. He was a great dad—conscientious and loving. He was overjoyed when he learned I'd gone to rehab and supportive when I got out. He called often. The initial rapport that we had once enjoyed was returning. I had reason to hope that reconciliation was possible. I wanted to put it all back together again. But events conspired to keep that from happening. Marvin married a woman who, in my view, was not worthy of him.

Then the call came. On March 22, 1985, I was in my dressing room in Dallas, getting ready for a show, when I was told that Marvin had died of a stroke. He was thirty-four. I'll never understand why I was told before, and not after, the show. To make it through, I had to share the tragic news with the audience. Afterward, I immediately asked Drue to fly Robbie to Dallas, where I told my seven-year-old son that his dad was gone.

My friends worried that the tragedy would throw me, newly sober, back into addiction. God knows I wanted to anesthetize the pain. By then, though, I knew that drugs were no longer an option. My responsibility was to our son, to rebuilding our life and regaining a career I had nearly thrown away. I prayed for strength. Prayer prevailed, and I was able to stay on the straight and narrow.

Slowly I found a footing. I began recording again and, thankfully, my fans responded enthusiastically. By then I had moved Aunt Bay and Janice to Los Angeles so we could all stay close. Eight months later—it was still 1985—Janice died of a stroke. She was also in her thirties.

Four years earlier, Janice and I had barely survived that frightening fire in the Vegas Hilton by walking down twenty-four smoke-filled stories. Because she was extremely heavy, the ordeal was especially injurious to Janice. She never fully recovered. At the same time, I was not prepared for Janice's sudden death.

Then sixteen months later, in March of 1987, Drue—

beautiful Drue who served as Robbie's nanny and my surrogate mom—also suffered a fatal stroke. When my aunt Bay passed, in 1994, I was similarly devastated; I lost one of the most loving people the world has ever known.

"When Marvin died," I told Cooke in September 2008, as I faced the prospect of flying to New York in my debilitated condition, "and then Janice and Drue died, I went through long periods of deep depression. I knew my life would always be poorer because of their absence. But then I told myself that my life would always be richer because of their presence. We spoke our love for each other all the time. Marvin and I had split up, but spiritually we had made up before he passed. I don't have to tell you, Cooke, that the pain of losing them never went away, but eventually the depression lifted. Now, though, with this physical shit I'm going through, the pain seems to be staying right in the center of my soul."

"Are you afraid, Sweetie?" asked Cooke.

"I'm not afraid that whatever I have will kill me. I'm more afraid that it *won't* kill me and I'll live the rest of a long life with this damn thing!"

Cooke's laugh was good medicine. Cooke's love was always my best medicine.

"Listen, Sweetie," she said, "I admire your never-say-die work ethic, and I know that work is sometimes the best antidote for what ails us. But I'm still worried about this New York trip. I still think you should skip it. Look what happened in Japan."

"Well, I did it, didn't I?"

"Barely."

"New York isn't as far as Tokyo."

"You're rationalizing."

"I'm working, Cooke. I gotta keep working till I feel better."

"And if you feel worse?"

"I can't imagine feeling much worse than I do now."

"I hope you're right, Sweetie."

I was wrong.

Long Nights

It was a Saturday afternoon when Jessica came over to my house. She had called beforehand, saying it was important. When she arrived, I could tell something was wrong. Jessica's eyes were usually smiling, but on this day they were sad.

"Where's Richard?"

"Solomon took him to a park to play."

"What's wrong?" I asked.

"I can tell you, Patty," she said, "because you're my sister. But I can't tell Mama—at least not now."

"What is it?"

"Solomon."

"What about him?"

"Well, it's about both him and me. We're breaking up. He's moving out."

I knew they were having problems but hadn't realized the problems were this severe.

"I'm sorry to hear that, Jessica."

"I've tried . . ."

"I know you have. But have you thought about a counselor?"

"He'd never go to a counselor. He wouldn't talk about our problems with a stranger. Never."

"Have you told Richard?"

"That's the part that's breaking my heart. It'll make him so sad. It's made *me* so sad. I haven't been able to sleep. It's like there's a dark cloud over my head."

"*Hermanita*," I told my sister, "I think you need help. You're normally the most cheerful person I know. This is hitting you hard. You're depressed, and I wish you'd see someone."

"Like a psychologist?"

"Or a psychiatrist."

"I don't know any."

"I do. I work in a hospital, remember?"

"What is a psychologist going to do for me?"

"You can talk about what's bothering you."

"I can do that with you."

"Psychologists are trained to guide you out of depression. And psychiatrists can prescribe medicines. Sometimes medicines can lift your spirits."

"Will you go with me?"

"Of course."

"And you'll tell Mama about me and Solomon breaking up."

"You'll tell her when you're ready."

"She'll be disappointed, won't she?" said Jessica.

"She'll understand."

"You always understand, Patty. I don't know what I'd do without you."

8

I'D DONE THE media morning talk show circuit many times before. I always enjoyed the experience. It's like downing a dozen double shots of espresso. The high is heady. You get up in the middle of the night, your wardrobe and makeup people arrive while it's still dark, your engines start churning, and before you know it, you're running from one TV appearance to the next, selling your latest product. It's all part of the game, and, as a professional, I took pride in doing it well.

What had been fun and energizing, though, was now absolute torture. Cooke was right. It was a trip I should not have made. On that fateful morning when I was scheduled to do three shows, I could barely lift my head off the pillow, get dressed, and keep from collapsing while I was driven to the studios.

Harry Smith on *The Early Show* could not have been sweeter. I talked about *Still Unforgettable* and, when asked, told the truth about how I had contracted hep C. When Harry asked how I was feeling, I lied. "Fine," I said.

Next, *The View*. Barbara, Whoopi, and Joy could not have been more understanding. I was scheduled to perform. For a quick second I thought of backing out, but half-dead as I might have been, I decided to brave it out. Miraculously, I came to life when I sang. Later, friends said they couldn't even tell I was hurting.

Off to *Today*, where Kathie Lee Gifford and Hoda Kotb were also great. Their questions were gentle, and their support of my CD enthusiastic. But how I made it through the interview is still beyond me. My head was reeling. In the limo, riding over to the next show, Sirius radio, I fell asleep.

That evening I managed to honor a commitment I'd made to a designer friend. I attended his show followed by a reception on a yacht. By then I was unable to walk in heels; I was practically unable to walk at all. Back at the hotel, I could hardly breathe. I grew alarmed and called my doctor in California.

"Just prop up your head in bed," he said. "Don't recline in a flat position."

I collapsed into a fitful sleep, waking up every half hour or so, fighting for normal breath.

Next morning I was due at Borders for a CD-signing event. My friend Denise Rich, who lives in New York, called to see about me. We were to have dinner together that night.

"You sound horrible," she said. "I'm sending my doctor over to the hotel."

"You don't have to do that, Denise."

"It's done. Don't move till he gets there."

The doctor, Angelo Acquista, took one look at me and said, "I need to see you in my office."

In his office he took X-rays and tests. When he came back with the results, he was not happy.

"You need to go to the hospital . . . now."

"Now? Why? What's going on?"

"Without immediate hospital care, you run a strong risk of dying. Your kidneys are functioning at eight percent."

"I thought the problem was my liver."

"No, Miss Cole, your kidneys are on the verge of shutting down. We're bringing you in to Lenox Hill Hospital."

Now, here's a funny thing about women. Or at least this woman. I'm sitting across from a doctor who's just told me that I could expire at any minute and the first thing I think is, I must run back to my hotel room to make sure I have my clothes and makeup together. I'm worried about all this womanly stuff, not the fact that I'm at death's door.

"Send someone else for your things, Miss Cole," the doctor said sternly. "I'm sending you to the hospital."

"The hospital!" Cooke exclaimed when I found the strength to call her from Lenox Hill. "I'm booking a flight right now."

"I don't think I'm going to be here that long," I said.

"In the hospital or on the planet?" asked Cooke.

"Both. The trouble is my kidneys. There's a good chance they'll eventually fail and I'll be looking for a new one."

"The chemotherapy healed your liver while destroying your kidneys. Is that it, Sweetie?"

"They're not saying, but that's what I'm guessing."

"So they're talking dialysis."

"It's already begun. Along with a blood transfusion."

"Oh, baby, I am so sorry you have to go through this."

"We'll have a lot of laughs when I get home, Cooke. And that should be real soon."

It wasn't. My Lenox Hill stay lasted nearly two weeks. And then, upon release, the doctors said I was too weak to travel. So I stayed in Brooklyn with Carol and Selene, two dear friends who, without the least hesitancy, brought me into their home and devoted themselves to my rehabilitation. It was as though I had two mothers.

And believe me, it took the love of two mothers to deal

with my post-hospitalization stuff. God bless Carol and Selene, who put their lives on hold and, in caring for me, displayed a patience that was absolutely angelic.

And God bless Bob Krasnow. He was the record exec responsible for *Unforgettable . . . with Love.* Despite his own medical problems, he and his wife flew to New York and drove out to Brooklyn, just to sit in a little chair by the side of my bed and take my mind off my misery.

The last thing I wanted to do was dwell on my physical condition. Bob knew that. He's a great schmoozer, and in reminiscing about people in the business we both knew, he raised my spirits and had me think about happier times. For an hour or so, I could forget about being sick.

"Look, Natalie," he said, "let's forget our hospital stories. Let's talk about our heroes. How about Sinatra?"

Bob's tactic worked. My thoughts immediately left my aching limbs and went to the man I called Uncle Frank. I remembered doing his TV special back in 1977 when I'd just found out I was pregnant with Robbie. On several occasions, I was invited to his home in Beverly Hills and his compound in Palm Springs. But the most special moment was appearing on the same bill with Sinatra at the Fukuoka Dome in Tokyo. It was one of his last concerts.

I told Bob how Frank had invited me for dinner in his hotel suite in Japan. There were many guests, and he was seated at the end of a long table. He put me right next to him so he could tell me stories about my dad. For instance, when my father was sick in the hospital in Santa Monica, Sinatra showed up with Sammy Davis Jr. They snuck Dad out of his room and took him down the street for a drink at a bar. "No one was cooler than Nat 'King' Cole," he said. "No one."

"How did the shows go?" asked Bob.

"Not well. When he started singing 'The Lady Is a Tramp' and couldn't remember the lyrics, I realized something was wrong. He got lost doing 'My Way' and 'New York, New York,' his signature songs. Later I read that he had the beginnings of Alzheimer's, but at the time I didn't understand. When we flew back, Frank started hitting the Jack Daniel's. He became belligerent and began confronting members of his entourage. 'Who the hell are you?' he screamed. I thought he was joking, Bob, but he wasn't. You know Eliot Weisman, Sinatra's manager. Well, at this point Eliot said, 'Natalie, go in the back and take a nap. I don't want you to see this.' I slept until we landed in Hawaii. By then Frank had stopped the berating but had no idea why he was on the plane. His short-term memory was shot; he'd forgotten all about Tokyo. It was sad to witness, but I'll always be grateful for his kindness to me and the fact that we performed together."

"Him and your dad," said Krasnow. "Two class acts."

"Because She Needs One"

"Hey, Patty, how you doin'?"

"Fine, Jessica, how you doin', *hermanita*?"

"I'm all right. Just got a little problem, though."

"What's wrong?"

"I'm a little short on funds. I maxed out my credit card."

"Buying what?"

"A TV.' "

"You have a nice TV."

"Yes, but I bought one for my babysitter."

"Why would you do that?"

"Because she needs one."

"But, Jessica, why can't she buy her own TV?"

"She's too poor to afford one."

"You aren't exactly rich."

"But I have more than her. Beside, her parents are sick. She had to move back home with them. And it turns out they don't have a TV either."

"So you bought her one?"

"I just felt so bad for her, sis. Most nights she's home alone. She needs a little entertainment."

"Listen to me, Jessica. You can't be buying televisions for just anyone."

"She's not just anyone, Patty. She's a wonderful person. She's truly deserving."

"I'm sure she is."

"So I'm a little short this month."

"Don't worry about it. I'll loan you what you need."

"Thanks, Patty. Every time I go out, she takes good care of Richard. Now I feel like I need to take care of her."

"That's a beautiful thought, Jessica, but it still leaves you broke."

"No worries. I got my health, I got my son, and I met a new guy."

"Wow. You save the headline for last. What's his name?"

"Julio."

"Where'd you meet him?"

"At the sporting goods store where I've been working. He came in for an interview."

"He get the job?"

"He sure did."

"What's he like?"

"He's wonderful, Patty. Everything is wonderful."

9

I LOVE GOSPEL music. I consider all music of the heart God's music. Music elevates and inspires, but gospel music excites my soul. When Aunt Bay brought me to Jesus in Chicago, she brought me back into a family from which I had long been separated. My dad's people were praying people. His dad was a minister and his wife, my grandmother, who unfortunately I did not know well, was the first lady of their church. Aunt Bay carried the Cole tradition of beautiful faith in every step she took. She went to church not to be seen or to appear proper; she went to give God the praise—and she did so with all the full-gospel glory at her command. I followed her loving lead. The congregation of blood-washed believers demanded preaching that pulled no punches. The minister was steeped in old-school pastoring; the choir was trained in old-school singing. The celebration of God's goodness was unrestrained. It was passionate; it pulsated with the righteous rhythms of a God you could feel in every fiber of your body.

One of the songs I love most says, "If the Lord never does anything else for me, he's done enough." It talks about being blessed not just once or twice, but being blessed every day of our lives. I kept hearing that song, hearing that holy message—"He's Done Enough"—even as I realized that, due to my failing kidneys, my life would never be the same.

I wasn't angry, I didn't feel like a victim—hell, it was my dope addiction that created this mess anyway—but I did realize I'd need a whole lot of patience to deal with dialysis. It wasn't fun being at the hospital three times a week for treatment.

After the long medical episode in New York, I was back in L.A., where I prayed for simple patience and the fortitude to move ahead. Sometimes the patience was there; other times I found myself exasperated.

Kidneys can respond to treatment and regenerate. In my case, they didn't. My doctors at Cedars-Sinai Medical Center concluded that I'd need ongoing dialysis. Without it, my kidneys would shut down and I'd die. I was also told that eventually I'd need a transplant. There was no certainty that I could survive on dialysis past a given number of years. No one knew how many.

The treatment itself was arduous. They went into my jugular with a PIC line—a catheter—to draw blood. Eventually I was hooked up to a machine—it reminded me of a giant computer—that mimics the functions of the kidneys. It washed my blood, then pumped the clean blood back into my body. The idea of washing my blood reminded me of Jesus. As I sat through the treatment, a three-hour ordeal, I thought of how Aunt Bay had instructed me in the faith of Christ.

"His blood washes you clean," she had said. "His sacrifice means He has paid the price for you. You're forgiven, baby. You're a free woman."

"But if you only knew what I'd done, Aunt Bay, you wouldn't say that."

"I'm not saying it, sugar. God is. The God we serve is a forgiving God. The blood that He shed is your shelter. The blood is beautiful blood because it's healing blood. It's holy blood; it's cleansing blood."

I tried to think of that as the dialysis machine cleansed my human blood. I tried to be grateful, not only to God, but to the miracles of modern medicine that were keeping me alive.

• • •

It was around 5:00 p.m. when I'd get in the bathtub to luxuriate and call my sister Cooke. She'd be finishing up at her office and I'd be home from a dialysis treatment.

"How'd it go?" she asked.

"Oh, a regular party," I answered.

"Well, at least you're home. And I'm presuming that you're staying home."

"Wish I could."

"What do you mean, 'wish'? What's preventing you?"

"The road."

"Fuck the road, Sweetie. You got to stay still for a minute. You can't be running off in the middle of your treatments."

"I've been doing research, Cooke, and discovered that you can arrange for dialysis practically anywhere. I can start singing again in a few weeks."

"According to who?"

"The doctors."

"You bribe them with money or sex?"

I had to laugh. My sister was fierce. "Seriously," I said. "They say I can travel."

"And I say you're crazy."

"It'll do me good. Keep my mind off my half-baked kidneys."

"As long as the gigs are close by."

"I told my manager, Barbara Rose, who, by the way, has been my guardian angel, not to book anything farther away than Athens."

"Georgia?"

"Greece."

Now Cooke was laughing. "You're going overseas?"

"A short tour. London, Rome, Paris, Athens."

"My sister the masochist."

"Your sister the survivor. If my life revolves around nothing but dialysis three times a week, I'll lose it. I'll go nuts. Singing will focus me back on something I love. It'll take off the edge."

"It always has."

"And always will."

Getting back to work wasn't easy. It took a while to get my voice back in shape. Thanks to Seth Riggs, my great vocal coach, I was able to do so. I knew that singing wouldn't heal my kidneys—it seemed nothing would—but it would get me out of myself and into the stories of the songs.

At concerts and club dates, I was still working to perfect live versions of the material from *Still Unforgettable*. I was still losing myself in the culture of my masters—Ella, Sarah, Lena, Sammy, Frank, and Dad—while interjecting some of my old hits. God bless my fans because, come hell or high water, they kept showing up.

And I kept showing up for dialysis at the DaVita medical facility. Those people were great. When I was on the road, arrangements were made ahead of time.

Once, because I was there for another procedure, I had my dialysis at Cedars-Sinai. On that day, I was attended by a nurse who lifted my spirits. Her name was Esther Seever, and she was an absolute doll. She called everyone "honey" and "sweetheart." She did her work with such devotion that I couldn't help but love her. We connected.

How could I know that this very brief encounter was a critical link in a chain of remarkable events that would save my life?

10

TWELVE MONTHS EARLIER, I had been in church, praising God and thinking about a bright new year ahead. I had no idea that I was carrying a viral disease left over from an earlier chapter in my life, had no idea that the "cure" for my infected liver—interferon—might damage my kidneys, no idea that my damaged kidneys would shut down and require dialysis. I'd gone from extremely healthy to extremely sick in a matter of weeks. As I approached sixty, I saw that living with failing kidneys could not go on forever. I'd need a new organ. But the waiting list seemed interminably long and, even if one were available, there was no guarantee it would be a good match. The danger of postoperative rejection was real. So was the fact that without a healthy kidney, my life could be shortened dramatically.

And yet, thanks to the miraculous way in which the faith of Aunt Bay entered my soul and comforted my heart, my own faith never faltered. It wasn't that I didn't experience moments of agitation and aggravation. Undergoing dialysis three times a week, whether in Los Angeles or London, was a nuisance. My energy was still low, and I wondered whether I'd ever be my old self. I could harbor doubts and feel discouraged, but the dark negativity couldn't hold a candle to the dazzling light of God's positive love. The dark clouds were there, but they passed quickly, and my life went forward.

I worked; I went to the hospital for my treatments; I stayed steady.

In February 2009, Cooke and I went see a photography exhibit in Santa Monica called Ashes and Snow. The artist, Gregory Colbert, presented a striking vision of animals, fish, and small children juxtaposed in images creating a kind of pure and innocent poetry. We were moved to the point of tears.

"There's a Zen calmness about these pictures," said Cooke. "It's amazing how he's brought harmony to elements that don't seem at all harmonious."

"It's the spirit of love," I said. "I think it's love that brings harmony to everything."

• • •

A month later, Cooke and I met at a party for *Re: Generations,* her pet project. She was the executive producer of a record she had developed with Capitol Records, a CD in which Nat Cole songs were resculpted and remixed by young musicians.

"It's a way to keep his music alive and available to a younger generation," she had told me.

"I like it," I said. "And I'm glad you're doing it, Cooke. No one else could do it any better."

"Except for Kelly."

"Well, I know our brother's spirit is right there with you."

The minute I arrived at the release party, I felt Kelly's spirit. It was a happy family occasion. A good-sized contingent of the Cole clan attended. Hearing "Mona Lisa" and "Those Lazy Hazy Crazy Days of Summer" funked-up on a hip-hop tip was fun. Everyone seemed in good form.

When I saw John, Cooke's longtime companion and soul mate, I asked, "Where's my sister?"

"She's sitting down over there," he said pointing to a chair.

"She okay?" I asked John.

"Just a little tired."

I waved to Cooke. She gave me a smile and waved back. I went over, bent down to kiss her on the cheek, and said,

"How come you're not working the crowd? This is your party."

"Just catching my breath, Sweetie," she said. "I'll be up in a minute."

And she was, going around to greet everyone with a big charming smile. I left a little before Cooke. Thinking of my sister, I felt blessed to have this wonderful woman in my life. As far I could tell, Cooke was fine.

Beautiful News

I was driving home from my job at the hospital. It was in the early months of 2009. It had been a particularly long day, and I was tired. Arturo and I and the kids were also in the process of moving to another house. There was lots of work to do. When my cell rang, I saw it was Jessica and answered right away.

"Hi, honey," I said. "Everything okay?"

"Everything's great, Patty. Fact is, I've got great news. Beautiful news."

"Found a job?"

Jessica had been searching for a while with no luck.

"Even better."

"The lottery?"

"Better!"

"Well, tell me."

"You're gonna be an aunt again."

Silence.

"You hear me?" asked Jessica.

"Sure, I heard you, *hermanita*, I'm just . . . just a little surprised."

"I'm surprised, too, but I couldn't be happier."

"Does Richard know that he's gonna have a little brother or sister?"

"Not yet. You're the first to know."

"You're telling me before you tell Mama?"

"*I always* tell you, Patty, before I tell Mama. I'm not too anxious to tell Mama. Mama's gonna be all worried."

"I gotta say, Jessica, that I'm a little worried."

"What's to worry about?"

"Well, you and Julio aren't married. You aren't even living together."

"Soon as the baby is born, we will be. We've already started looking for a place."

"And Julio is happy about this?"

"He's thrilled," said Jessica. "He wants us to have a child. He wants a family."

"I realize that, but you haven't divorced Solomon yet."

"That's just a technical thing. That's just because of Richard. Richard likes the idea that his mom and dad, even though they don't live together, are married. But we'll get the divorce. It'll all happen in due time. Meanwhile, Patty, I want you to be happy for me. I'm thirty-two years old. I found the man of my dreams. I'm ready to have another baby. I really am."

"Do you have a due date?"

"June tenth."

"When are you going to tell Mama?"

"There's no hurry. I can wait."

"Not too long you can't."

"You can help me with that, Patty, can't you?"

"Sure. I'll have Arturo cook a family barbecue next month. Mama loves those barbecues. We'll all be together, and it'll be a good time to tell her the news."

"The beautiful news."

"Yes, Jessica, it is beautiful news."

What a Blessing!

I could see that Jessica was nervous. She came to dinner with her eleven-year-old son, Richard, a great kid. Aunt Tete is also great, and so are my sons, Christopher and Jonathan, who, at nineteen and twenty-one, are handsome young men. And, of course, Mama, the spiritual heart of our family, was there, happy to see us all together.

Arturo and I prepared the enchiladas, beans, tacos, and tamales. Arturo was barbecuing the carne asada. The March evening was mild and we were all in the backyard, sipping our drinks and waiting for the meat to cook. It smelled wonderful.

I kept looking at Jessica, indicating it was time to tell Mama. But she kept talking about other things. I took her to the side of the yard, away from everyone.

"Isn't it hot to be wearing a sweater?" I asked her.

"If I take it off, Mama will see I'm pregnant. I've begun to show."

"Jessica, Mama needs to know."

"I'm not ready. I'm gonna wait another month."

"In another month you'll *really* be showing. That's no way for Mama to find out."

"Then you tell her."

"You're making too much of this, *hermanita*," I said. "We'll have dinner, we'll serve dessert, we'll all be in a good mood—and then, at the end of the evening, you'll make your announcement."

"Okay."

After our whispering, we went to rejoin the family. That's when, out of nowhere, Jessica blurted out, "Mama, you're going to be a grandmother again!"

Mama was stunned. I was a little stunned because I expected that Jessica would wait till later. Later she told me this was the only way she could do it.

I had to pretend that I was surprised. I didn't want Mama to know that her daughter had told me before her.

"That's wonderful!" I said. "What a blessing!"

For a long time, Mama said nothing. Her silence was loud. I chimed in, asking about the due date, even though I knew it was June 10. Arturo said something nice about Richard having a little brother or sister. My sons, who loved their aunt, were happy to hear the news.

"Another baby is expensive," said Mama.

"Julio has a good job," said Jessica.

"But you aren't living with Julio," said Mama. "You aren't married to Julio."

Julio wasn't there that night. Jessica knew his presence would make her announcement even more difficult.

"Julio and I will be living together. We'll get married after our baby's born."

"And what about Richard's father? When are you going to see about divorcing Solomon?"

"That will happen in due course, Mama. Solomon and I are on good terms. He's a great dad."

More silence from Mama.

"You've been laid off from your job," said Mama. "I worry about the financial strain."

"We'll make it," said Jessica.

"We'll all help," I said.

Mama just sat there. We could all feel her concern. She was worried about her baby daughter, worried about Jessica's domestic and financial situation. Mama was worried about everything.

When the carne asada was ready, we went to the dining room table. We blessed the food and dug in.

"The carne asada is delicious," Aunt Tete told Arturo.

Mama ate without saying a word. My sons, both champion swimmers, talked about their work as lifeguards. I mentioned something funny that had happened at my job at the hospital. Aunt Tete, a nurse, had a few funny stories of her own. It was all very pleasant. Except that Mama didn't join in.

Finally, after dessert, Mama spoke. She turned to Jessica and asked, "What will you be needing for the new baby?"

"A crib, Mama. I really need a good crib."

"I'll get you a crib, *niña*. You pick out whatever you want."

And with that, Mama opened her arms to her Jessica, and they embraced.

11

I KNOW BOB Dylan has gone through many religious changes, and I'm not sure what his current status is. I do know, though, that he wrote a song called "Gotta Serve Somebody," and when he learned I was going to record it, he added some extra lyrics. Whether that was because he knew I was a believer or not, I can't say. All I can say is that I'm grateful to Mr. D. and I love the song.

I believe the message. Whether we like it or not, we're all servants. We're serving a higher power or a lower one. Out of selfishness, we serve ourselves first; out of generosity, we first serve others. We serve patience or we serve impetuosity. We serve up portions of compassionate love or ingredients of fearful greed.

On Mother's Day, May 10, 2009, I understood the urgency with which I had to serve my sister. That urgency came as a shock.

At first it didn't look like I'd be able to spend Mother's Day with Cooke. I was in Seattle and on my way to Seoul, Korea. Then, providentially, the Korean date was canceled. That allowed me to fly back to L.A.

On May 9, the day before Mother's Day, Sage, Cooke's son, had called me. I'd just arrived home from the airport.

"Sweetie," he said, "I just want you to know that Mom is really sick."

"Sick? What's wrong?"

"John had to take her to the hospital. I don't know the details."

"Which hospital?"

"The one in Tarzana."

"I'm going to try to reach John now."

"No one wanted me to call you," Sage said. "They thought you'd get too upset. But I felt that you needed to know right away."

"You were right. Thank you."

A flurry of calls went back and forth. I really wanted to speak with my sister but understood that I couldn't. She was being examined. I then learned she was being released and would be home that night. The next day, Mother's Day, I drove to her house.

When I walked through the door, Cooke came walking toward me. My heart went cold. Always plump, Cooke had lost a drastic amount of weight. When we embraced, she felt slight in my arms, weak. Her complexion was ashen. I had seen that look before.

I brought flowers and her favorite soul food—macaroni and cheese, collard greens, corn bread—but when we sat down to eat, she hardly took a bite.

"No appetite," she said. "Think I better rest for a minute. Come rest with me, Sweetie."

I followed her into the bedroom. I noticed that her Buddhist shrine was in its usual place, but I also noticed copies of *The Daily Word*, a book of Christian meditations.

She got into bed and I climbed in next to her.

"What is it, Cooke? What did the doctor say?"

"They don't know yet. They just took tests. But enough about me. Tell me about your dialysis treatments. How are you tolerating them?"

I didn't want to discuss my health; I was far too worried about Cooke's. But I could see she wanted to take her mind off herself.

"The treatments seem to be working. I don't have to tell you that they're boring as hell. You just sit and sit."

"Can you read?"

"I read, I watch a little TV, I text, but it's still monotonous."

"And how's it working when you're out of town?"

"Management has been great. They make arrangements to hook me to the monster machine no matter where I am."

"And what about the transplant possibilities?"

"Not a word."

"You don't ask?"

"I figure they'll tell me if a match shows up."

Cooke started to say something but began having problems breathing.

I grew alarmed. "You okay?"

She caught her breath and said, "Fine. Just tired."

I wanted to ask more about her condition, but she was too exhausted to be cross-examined.

"Why don't you sleep a little?" I suggested.

"Done nothing but sleep for a week straight," she said.

With that, Cooke closed her eyes. After she had fallen asleep, I tiptoed out of the room.

John and I went to his study, where we sat down and I peppered him with questions. He told me that the first sign had been her swollen stomach. That had been evident six months ago. The pain was severe, but all this time she was determined to keep her malady to herself. As the great matriarch of her family, she didn't want to alarm anyone. For a long while, she had refused to go to the doctor. When the suffering became unbearable, she had acquiesced.

"Even then," said John, "I practically had to force her. You know how she feels about Western medicine."

"I know."

"And she especially didn't want you to know."

"When will we have the test results?"

"Day after tomorrow. We're meeting with the doctor back in the hospital."

"I'm coming with you."

"She might protest," said John, "but I know she'd like you to be there."

Mother's Day, May 10, 2009

Jessica came to my house with a bouquet of roses and a lovely card.

Her card, which I still cherish, read:

Patty, as we've grown older, it's been interesting to discover how alike we are in some ways, and how different we are in others. I just want you to know there's someone who knew you then . . . and loves you now. Con mucho cariño, *Jessica.*

I thanked her for the card and flowers and asked how she was feeling.

"Fine," she said.

Given her condition, she looked a little thin to me. I also noticed that her feet were swollen. I had noticed the same thing a week ago at the baby shower Julio had given her. It had been a joyous day—friends, family, and presents—yet I couldn't help but be a little concerned.

I had mentioned the swelling to Jessica then, and on Mother's Day I mentioned it again.

"I don't think it's anything," she said.

"Be good to go to the doctor and check it out," I said.

"Do you really think so?"

"Yes."

"You work in a hospital, Patty," she said. "You're conditioned to worry about everyone's health."

"It's probably nothing, but it's best to be sure."

"I've had such a healthy pregnancy," Jessica reminded me. "I really haven't stopped for a minute."

She was right. During the pregnancy, Mama, who had suffered a fall in a grocery store, initiated a lawsuit, and Jessica had driven her to a long series of meetings in the lawyer's office. What's more, Jessica had helped Aunt Tete and had also given me and Arturo a hand fixing up our new house. We were careful to make sure that she didn't strain herself, but we couldn't keep her away from all the activity. As usual, she wanted to be helpful—and was.

"I'm not one of those pregnant women who can sit around, eat candy, and watch TV," she said. "I need to stay active."

"Well, you've been super-active. And you don't have long to go."

"The last weeks are the hardest."

"You and Julio still don't want to know your baby's sex?" I asked.

"We want to be surprised. But I think it's a boy. What's your guess, Patty?"

"A boy, but I'm rarely right about these things."

"Be beautiful for Richard to have a little brother."

"Or a little sister, *hermanita*," I suggested.

"I know how wonderful it is to have a sister," said Jessica, squeezing my hand.

"Me, too."

For a minute or two, we sat in silence.

"You will go see the doctor about your feet?"

"Not if you don't stop nagging me."

"I'll stop."

"Then I'll go."

For the rest of Mother's Day, with our children by our sides, we did nothing but eat, talk, and laugh.

12

THE IMPACT OF losing my dad at age fifteen was incalculable. Some twenty years later, while in rehab, I was told by a wise counselor that I still hadn't mourned the loss. I'm not sure I ever will. My teenage years will forever be defined by my father's death.

I had known Cooke, however, four times longer than I had known my dad. I had never known life without her. I couldn't imagine life without her. Seeing the gravity of her condition filled me with anxiety. I couldn't lose my sister. I just couldn't.

This shocking turn of events threw me. I had to stay

steady or I'd be of no use to anyone, so I turned to prayer. I didn't pray out of a belief that by petitioning God we change God's will. I prayed because I didn't know what else to do. In prayer I feel God's presence. While my head is spinning and my soul storming, prayer calms me, if only for a moment or two. Like everyone, I am tempted to beseech God to protect and save my loved ones, and if those thoughts come spilling out, that's only human. But more than pleading with God, my prayer was for Cooke to feel His goodness and be comforted by His grace. My prayer was that His love blanket all of us as we face challenges both unexpected and frightening.

Driving to the hospital, though, I was very frightened. When I saw Cooke, I acted bravely. I helped sign her in and went with her to an examination room, where they took tissue from her breast for further study.

Then we waited.

"Nervous?" she asked me.

"No more than you," I said.

She took my hand and said, "I guess it's okay for us to be scared as hell."

"Damn right. Hospitals are always scary."

The wait continued. It seemed interminable. My sister and I made chitchat, but her energy was low and our apprehension grew by the minute. Finally, we were told to go to the doctor's office. John and Cooke's son Harleigh were already there.

The doctor spoke plainly, directing his words to Cooke.

"The tests are conclusive. There are spots on your lungs," he said.

My heart dropped.

He continued. "There are also spots on your pancreas and gallbladder. I strongly recommend that we begin chemotherapy within twenty-four hours."

He never used the word *cancer.* He didn't have to.

Cooke was deeply shaken by the doctor's report but able to maintain her composure.

"Are there homeopathic alternatives to chemotheraphy?" she asked.

"There are," said the doctor, "but at this stage I would very much doubt their efficacy. This is no time for experimentation."

"I need to think about it."

"I understand. But I must repeat—I'd like to initiate chemotherapy by tomorrow at the latest."

"I'll consider it."

I knew my sister. No matter how strongly the doctor urged such treatments, she would never agree.

"I also want you to stay in the hospital tonight," he added, "because your sodium level is dangerously low. We must give you an infusion."

Cooke agreed to stay.

"You don't have to stay with me, Sweetie," she told me.

"John and Harleigh are here. I'll be fine. It's just one night and I'll be home tomorrow."

I called that night to learn that, according to John, the procedure had gone well.

"They're releasing her tomorrow morning," said John.

"And the chemotherapy?" I asked, already knowing the answer.

"She's ruled it out."

"Please call me as soon as you bring her home."

The next day it was Cooke who called.

"I'm home," she said.

"How are you doing?"

"Much better. Actually feeling good."

"I'm so glad, Cooke. This weekend is my goddaughter's graduation in Atlanta. I want to cancel the trip and spend the time with you . . ."

"Don't be silly, Sweetie. You need to go. I'll be fine."

"I feel funny about leaving you."

"I'm telling you, Sweetie—I'm okay. Go to Atlanta."

I went, but my sister stayed on my mind every minute of the day.

That was Friday, May 15.

Friday, May 15, 2009

This was the day Jessica was going to see the doctor about her swollen feet. I knew the appointment was in the morning, so when I didn't hear from her by three or four, I started to worry. After her doctor's appointment, she always called me.

At about five o'clock, I called her cell, but she didn't pick up.

Finally, at seven, Julio, her boyfriend, called me.

"What happened at the doctor's?" I asked.

"He admitted her to the hospital."

"Great!" I said. "The baby's coming a few weeks early."

"I don't know anything," Julio said, his voice sounding uncertain and afraid, "but I need to call your mother."

"Why?"

"She needs to be here. You need to be here."

"What's going on, Julio? Why all the alarm?"

"I don't know. They won't tell me anything."

"Is she having the baby? Is something wrong?"

"Just come now, Patty, and bring your mother. I think Jessica's mother needs to be here."

"Let me talk to Jessica."

"You can't. They've put a tube in her."

"Did they specify a reason for the tube?"

"Patty, I don't understand what's happening. I just know it isn't good."

I tried to get more information from Julio, but he was barely able to keep it together. I knew I had to get Mama and rush to the hospital.

The only car available had a stick shift—which I can't drive—so I had to borrow my son's girlfriend's car. I ran over and picked up Mama, who lived close to the Kaiser hospital in the San Fernando Valley, where Jessica had been admitted.

Mama asked me the same questions I had asked Julio.

"No one is saying anything at this point," I said. "We won't know until we get to the hospital."

When we got to the hospital, though, we still didn't know. The mystery continued, and we were beside ourselves with worry. Julio was there, along with his mom and one of his sisters, but they had not been able to talk to the attending physician. Finally, sometime after ten o'clock, a doctor appeared.

"I'm the sister, and this is the mother," I said. "We're desperate to know what's going on."

"We're looking for a neurologist."

"Why?" I asked.

"Because this hospital doesn't have one."

"But why a neurologist?"

"She's suffered a hemorrhage."

Mama started crying. I held my breath, fought for composure, began asking more questions.

I learned that the baby, a boy, had been delivered. The baby was fine. But what about my sister?

That's when the doctor used the word *preeclampsia*. He explained that it occurs in the late stages of pregnancy. The only possible remedy is to deliver the baby. But that is no guarantee that the mother will be all right. Preeclampsia is characterized by excessive protein in the urine. The blood pressure can elevate to extreme levels. The results can be catastrophic.

"Will my sister survive this?" I had to ask.

The doctor hesitated for a second. Then he said, "I don't know."

13

My goddaughter's graduation in Atlanta on Saturday, May 16, was beautiful. She's a lovely young woman whose accomplishment was great cause for celebration. I tried to stay present; I congratulated her and her family; I went to the dinners and the parties; I was there, but I really wasn't. My heart and mind were with my sister in California.

I called Cooke Saturday night.

"I knew it was you," she said.

I laughed. "How could you tell?"

"The phone had that worried ring to it."

"You doing all right?" I asked.

"I'm not entering a marathon today, but I'm getting by."

"That's the spirit."

"When will I see you, Sweetie?"

"Soon as I get back. Monday is my dialysis. I'll be over right after that."

"Love you, Sweetie."

"Love you, too, Cooke."

I had no idea that this would be the last time I'd hear my sister's voice.

Saturday, May 16, 2009

The corridor outside Jessica's ICU was so crowded with family and friends that the nurses couldn't pass by. There were old people, young people, nieces, nephews, crying babies. It was as though we had taken over the hospital. The number of people who came to pray for Jessica was amazing.

Eventually her son Richard arrived with his father, Solomon. They were both devastated. Aunt Tete was there, holding up as best she could. Mama and I had been up all night, frantic for news. Had they been able to stop the hemorrhaging? Had they found a neurologist? What in God's name was happening?

Finally, early Saturday morning, the doctor appeared. He asked that we follow him to a private room. I knew this was not a good sign. Mama, Julio, Julio's mom, Aunt Tete, and I sat down as he began to speak. I braced myself.

His explanation was long and confusing. He spoke of the traumatic impact of the hemorrhage and the severity of Jessica's coma. His language was technical. I grew frustrated and said, "Doctor, I don't understand what you're saying. Please be plain."

He waited a second or two before saying, "Jessica is brain dead."

I could hold back no longer. I burst into tears. I tried to get up and go to Mama. I wanted to comfort her. But as I stood, my knees buckled.

My mother was confused. She wanted to know the difference between "brain dead" and simply "dead."

We were told that Jessica was being kept alive by machines, but her brain was no longer functioning. The doctor showed us the CT scan. He said that two different neurologists had done the evaluation, and they both came to the same conclusion. They had all decided to disconnect her.

"You can't do that!" I cried. "Maybe the tests are wrong."

"The tests are not wrong," the doctor insisted.

"That's my baby sister in there! I won't let you kill her without absolute proof that there is no chance of recovery!"

"The CT scans prove exactly that," the doctor said.

"I can't read a CT scan! I can't take a chance that the scan is wrong or that the doctors read it wrong! I can't let you do this to my sister! I just can't!"

It had happened too quickly, it was too unbelievable for me to accept. Only hours ago Jessica was alive and well. Now they were telling me she was dead.

"The hospital has the right to disconnect her," the doctor said.

"You have no right! I won't allow it!"

Another doctor arrived at that moment—Jessica's obstetrician-gynecologist—and suggested that, as a compromise, we transfer Jessica to Providence, the hospital where she had been scheduled to deliver. Another evaluation by a completely different group of doctors.

"Yes!" I exclaimed. "Transfer her! Take her to another hospital!"

"We can't be certain whether, at this stage, they'll accept her," the doctor said.

"They will!" I cried. "They have to! They have to save my sister!"

Sunday, May 17, 2009

"I'm sorry," the doctor said at 7:00 a.m., "but the deadline has passed, and Providence won't accept your sister."

"On what grounds?" I asked.

"They feel her case is hopeless."

"Did your staff influence them?"

"No. Providence made their decision independently."

I fell into Mama's arms and cried for a long while. We had been up for three days, and I was beyond exhaustion, beyond grief. Everything was one big blur. I couldn't think, couldn't do anything but weep.

Finally, the doctor spoke. There was compassion in his voice. "There is one last test we can do before disconnecting her."

"Please explain," said Mama.

"We can unplug her from the ventilator for ten minutes. The ventilator is doing the breathing for her. If, during those ten minutes, she cannot breathe on her own, that becomes further conclusive proof that she is dead."

"Is that okay with you, Patty?" Mama asked.

I didn't know what to else to feel, do, or say. So I said, "Yes, that's okay."

Julio and I went to the room where the test was to be done while Mama stayed behind. We just sat there, watching the doctor disconnect Jessica from the machines. Ten minutes seemed like ten years. Every second was an eternity. The clock on the wall sat right above our heads. It was an old-fashioned clock that made a sound. Tick tock. Tick tock. Tick tock.

The doctor continually checked my sister's breathing. Finally, the ten minutes expired; the doctor's eyes told me all I needed to know. His eyes said my sister was gone.

"I'm sorry," he said. "She is unable to breathe on her own. There are no more tests we can run. There are no other alternatives. I'm afraid that we've exhausted every possibility. Legally, we are constrained from reconnecting Jessica to the machine. We are declaring her officially dead."

Officially dead.

The words were knives through my heart.

For thirty-two years, she had been officially alive, beautifully alive, alive in every sense of the word. For thirty-two years, she had been happy, healthy, filled with optimism and love. For thirty-two years, she had carried a carefree spirit. She had waltzed her way through life. And then one day her feet were swollen and some hours later, she was officially dead.

Officially dead.

I tried to drum the expression out of my mind but couldn't. It was so definite, so absolute, so forever.

"You must make some decisions," the doctor said.

"I realize that."

When we recently lost my mother's mom, we decided on cremation. It was an expensive procedure. My mother had little money. Arturo and I were just scraping by. I knew the same was true of Solomon and Julio. I didn't want to beg anyone to pay for funeral arrangements.

But far more important to me was this notion: Jessica was a giver. Jessica lived to help others. That was her main passion in life. Why shouldn't her spirit be honored? Because she was young and healthy, her organs might be transplanted to others, even to the point of saving lives.

The idea moved from my head to my heart. It warmed my heart. I saw it as a way of keeping Jessica alive in other people. But what would my mother, a far more traditional woman than I, think? I hesitated before mentioning it. After all, Mama had just been told that her baby was "officially dead." At the same time, I knew that a decision had to be made. I closed my eyes, offered a short prayer up to God, and said, "Mama, I think we should donate Jessica's organs."

Mama looked at me. There was so much pain in that look. She didn't answer for a while, but when she did, her voice was calm and certain.

"Jessica would like that," she said.

"I'll have a representative from OneLegacy come see you," said the doctor. "He'll take care of everything. For now, though, you and your family may want to tell Jessica good-bye."

"Yes," I said, "we want to see her one last time."

Mama went in first. Alone. She stayed for several minutes.

Arturo and my boys went next. When they came out, they were openly weeping.

Solomon took Richard, the son born to him and Jessica, so Richard could tell his mother good-bye.

Julio went to see her as well. He was comforted by his mother, sister, and brothers.

I was the last. I was shaking. I opened the door and saw Jessica in a way I had never seen her before. She looked beautiful. She looked angelic. Her skin was pure white. Her cheeks were rosy, her lips a natural shade of red. She appeared peaceful. I thought of Sleeping Beauty.

She's asleep, I thought to myself. She's resting. But soon she will be intertwined into the lives of others. Soon she will be awakened and have new adventures, new purpose. Soon she will be happy because she will be helping. Soon she will be living again.

That afternoon, Eric, the gentleman from OneLegacy, came to see me and Mama. Aunt Tete was with us. Eric was patient and compassionate. He had beautiful manners and could not have been more sensitive. He explained that, given Jessica's youth and strong body, many of her organs could be utilized. Our attitude was straightforward. Following Jessica's spirit, we wanted to help as many people as possible.

"Wonderful," said Eric. "At this point there's every reason to believe we will be able to successfully transplant her heart, liver, pancreas, corneas, and both kidneys."

I could see that the naming of the actual body parts took its toll on Mama. But Mama hung in. We were both convinced—then and now—that we were following Jessica's will.

"Do you have anyone in mind to whom you want to donate organs?"

"I don't," I said.

"Neither do I," said Mama.

"I do," said Aunt Tete.

"Aunt Tete works at Cedars-Sinai," I told Eric.

"I have patients in great need of kidneys. I love all three of them, and I'd love to help them. They are wonderful people whose lives depend on a new kidney," Aunt Tete said.

In this dark, dark period, I suddenly saw a beam of light—Jessica saving lives.

14

MONDAY MORNING, MAY 18, I was still in Atlanta. I got up and had a quick breakfast. Just as the bellman came to get my bags, the phone rang.

It was John, asking when I'd be back home. I told him I was getting ready to catch a flight. I'd be leaving right away.

"Cooke passed out early this morning," he said, "and I'm taking her back to the hospital."

I caught my breath, left the hotel, got in the car, and arrived at the airport an emotional wreck. The plane ride seemed interminable. I went over everything, all these sudden developments in Cooke's condition. Then I remembered my own condition—that I was due for dialysis later in the day at Cedars-Sinai.

My dear cousin Pam met me at the airport. I immediately called John.

"She's better," he said, "but we're still at the hospital."

Do I go to dialysis or go see my sister? I decided to go to dialysis. That way I'd be able to spend the rest of the day with Cooke.

Pam accompanied me to the medical facility. A nurse hooked me up to the monster machine that started washing my blood.

It wasn't more an hour later when Pam got a call on her cell. By Pam's expression, I could see it wasn't good news.

"What's wrong?" I asked.

"It's Cooke," she said. "Cooke's slipped into a coma."

"Please unhook me now!" I told the nurse. "I've got to go!"

We raced over the hill to the Valley. On the way, I stayed on the phone and learned that the coma was grave, her conditional critical. I spoke to my mother and sisters Casey and Timolin. They were crying. They were buying plane tickets to fly in from Florida. The world was spinning. I had to get to Cooke.

John and Cooke's sons were by her side. So was her beautiful grown daughter, Caroline, whom Cooke had had to give up for adoption. After many years, they had rediscovered each other and forged a great relationship. My son, Robbie, was also there, along with dozens of others, old and young, aunts, uncles, cousins, nieces, nephews, godchildren, and friends. The hospital was overflowing with people who loved Cooke.

I sat on the bed and looked at Cooke's face. I knew I was losing her. I held her hand, stroked her cheek, and prayed, "Not this, Lord. Please, not my Cooke."

That afternoon, sitting by Cooke's side, I had no concept of time, no concept of anything except staying with my sister. All concentration was on her.

Robbie came over to me, holding out his cell phone. "Mom, it's for you. It's a nurse from Cedars-Sinai."

"I can't talk to any nurse."

"She says it's absolutely urgent."

Reluctantly, I took the phone.

"Miss Cole?" she said.

"Yes."

"This is Jennifer from the transplant center at Cedars-Sinai. We have just received notification that a kidney has been designated for you. The organ isn't here yet, but it appears to be a perfect match. We want to schedule a transplant as soon as possible."

Well, how could she know that my sister was lying there,

dying right in front of me? But I went off anyway and said, "Look, I can't talk to you right now. I'll have to call you back."

And with that, I hung up the phone.

Monday, May 19, 2009

The phone rang in the early afternoon.

"Patty, it's Eric from OneLegacy. Sorry to bother you, but I must ask you a question."

"I thought we filled out all the papers authorizing the transplants."

"You have. This is another matter. I must ask how you know Natalie Cole?"

"Natalie Cole?" I thought about the name, searched my brain. But, in truth, I didn't know who that was.

"I don't know a Natalie Cole."

"I do not mean to offend you, Patty, but I must ask if Natalie Cole has offered you any money. Because if she has, I'm afraid that goes against our policy of..."

I was taken aback. "Eric," I said, "no one offered us anything. Not a dime. And besides, who is Natalie Cole?"

"One of the women you named to receive a transplant."

"That was Aunt Tete, not me. Aunt Tete is a nurse, and she said there were women in her dialysis unit whom she loved. She wanted to help them. That's it."

"Are you certain?"

"Absolutely."

"Then I take you at your word."

I hung up the phone, still bothered by the question. Why would anyone question our motives in donating these organs? After a few minutes, I settled down. I realized that there must be people who do this sort of thing for mercenary purposes. I rethought my purpose and came to the same conclusion I'd reached when the subject first came up—I wanted to keep Jessica alive through the lives of others.

I called Mama.

"Mama, have you ever heard of Natalie Cole?"

"Of course. She's the daughter of Nat 'King' Cole. He was a famous singer who had many hit recordings. He even sang in Spanish. His daughter is a singer as well."

"When Aunt Tete mentioned that she had patients who needed kidneys, did you know that one of them was Natalie Cole?"

"No."

"Well, one of them is Natalie Cole. OneLegacy called to make sure we weren't being paid for Jessica's kidney."

"That's ridiculous."

"That's what I told Eric."

"If Tete thinks she's a worthy person, though, I'm sure she is."

When I hung up the phone, I went to the computer and Googled Natalie Cole. On Wikipedia, I read some of her story. I saw that she had been born wealthy, but she had not had an easy life. She had been troubled by drug addiction and bad marriages. I wondered what she was really like.

Around midnight, Eric called back. He apologized for questioning our motives and then told me the news I had been expecting: they had begun to remove the various organs from Jessica's body.

A shiver went through me.

I took several breaths. Then my heart spoke to my sister and said, "Jessica, you are going on a new journey. You are going to have many new journeys. You are helping people in ways you could never have imagined."

15

It was two o'clock in the morning, Tuesday, May 19, when I left the hospital in Tarzana.

Cooke was holding on. I had to go home and get some sleep. I drove back over the hill to Los Angeles and my apartment on Wilshire Boulevard. I got in my pajamas, fell into bed, and collapsed into a deep but turbulent sleep.

The piercing ring of the phone woke me up. I was out of it, had no idea how long I'd been sleeping. It could have been a day; it could have been a week. It turned out it was only an hour. It was 3:00 a.m. On the line was a nurse from the hospital in Tarzana.

"I'm afraid that your sister has taken a turn for the worse. I think you should get back here."

That's all I needed to hear. I quickly got dressed and drove back over the hill.

Cooke was slipping. Her hold on life seemed frighteningly tenuous. I reestablished my position by her side. I held her hands, whispered words of encouragement. I still held hope that Cooke would make it.

Time stopped. Time passed. Somewhere around 4:30 a.m., my cell phone rang.

"Miss Cole," said the nurse from Cedars-Sinai, "I realize the difficult situation you are in. I know your sister is gravely ill. I have no choice, though, but to tell that if you are not here by six a.m., we will have to give this kidney, which is a perfect match for you, to someone else."

"Six a.m. this morning?"

"Yes, ninety minutes from now."

"I'll call you back."

"Please do. And quickly. If you're going to have this operation, I must make immediate arrangements."

"I understand."

I clicked off.

I looked around the room. My son. Cooke's family. Friends.

I didn't want to bother them with my dilemma.

How could I? My sister was in a coma, facing death. They were shocked and grieved and in no position to advise me.

I went into the hallway and thought for a second. I needed clarity, objectivity. I decided that at this moment the most levelheaded person I knew was Howard Grossman, my business manager. I called him.

"Howard, Cooke is in this horrible coma that she may not come out of. At the same time, Cedars is saying they have a perfectly matched kidney for me. What the hell should I do?"

"Do what Cooke would want you to do. Go for it."

"Are you sure?"

"Positive. Stop agonizing and just go for it."

I went back to Cooke, leaned over, and kissed her good-bye.

"I love you," I said. "I'll always love you."

From there, my cousin Pam and my friend Cecille drove back home with me. Tammy was waiting for me at the apartment. They quickly helped me pack a bag and, more important, helped me maintain my sanity.

It was a surreal moment.

The city streets were deserted. As we raced down Wilshire Boulevard toward Cedars-Sinai, the sun began its slow ascent. We arrived at the hospital a few minutes after six. Pam took away my cell phone.

Once in the hospital, even as I lay on my bed waiting for the transplant, death was something very far away. I just believed that Cooke would pull through.

When my surgeon, Dr. Louis Cohen, came into the room, he looked at me and said, "This is going to be very cool."

Who says that kind of stuff? In the midst of all this drama, I actually found the statement comforting. Cool statement, cool doctor.

As they wheeled me into the operating room, it was 3:00 p.m. My thoughts were on my sister.

Entertainment Tonight

I had gone to work on Tuesday, but my mind was on Jessica. I felt her absence in the pit of my stomach. Throughout the day, I was grieving so intensely that I had to leave my desk and go to the ladies' room, where I broke down.

That evening after dinner, after God knows how many long periods of weeping with Arturo holding me in his arms, I turned on the TV. I thought TV might distract me.

I was flipping the channels when, on an entertainment news show, I saw a picture of Natalie Cole. The broadcaster said, "Today in Los Angeles, Natalie Cole underwent a successful kidney transplant operation. Tonight she's resting quietly at Cedars-Sinai Hospital."

It had happened.

Jessica was alive in Natalie.

16

When I came out of recovery on Tuesday at 11:30 p.m., my family and friends were waiting for me. They were smiling, blowing me kisses, jubilant that I had survived the long and arduous operation. Dulled by heavy sedatives, I was still out of it, but their smiles registered. They were glad I was alive. I saw their beautiful faces but couldn't stay awake as I drifted off on another cloud of deep sleep.

It wasn't until Wednesday morning that I had an inkling of reality.

The doctor was there, along with Pam.

"The transplant was successful. You have a new and fully functioning kidney."

Those were the first words spoken by the doctor.

The next words were spoken by Pam.

"Cooke passed."

No, no, no . . . I couldn't believe it; didn't want to believe it. I wouldn't allow Pam's words to register.

Several seconds passed before I asked Pam to repeat what she had said.

"Sweetie," she said, "Cooke passed."

"When?" I asked.

"Yesterday."

"Before my operation?"

"Yes, yesterday morning at eight thirty."

"And no one told me?"

"The doctors told us not to. They didn't want you distraught. They said you needed all your strength for the transplant."

I closed my eyes to try to absorb the news. I couldn't. I didn't know how to feel grateful and grieve at the same time. I couldn't put the two elements together. As I gained life, Cooke lost hers. I cried so hard. It hurt so bad.

Pam took my hand. She understood.

The doctor said that the prognosis for my future was bright. He didn't understand. How could he? How could I face a future without Cooke? How could I deal with my good fortune while she, in a matter of a few short weeks, had been dealt a fortune of utter devastation?

Then, a blur of faces and voices:

My mother arrived. My beautiful younger sisters were also there. My son. Family, friends, a stream of well-wishers, so many people, in fact, that the hospital gave them a large room where they could congregate.

Imagine—the same huge gang of folks who had been at the hospital in Tarzana had, immediately after Cooke's passing, come to be with me at Cedars-Sinai. I could only imagine what was going through the mind of John, who had lost his partner, or the minds of Caroline, Sage, and Harleigh, who had lost their mom. To have them by my side, supporting me only hours after the tragedy they'd suffered, was testimony to their great strength of character and family devotion. What a transfer of emotion!

My mother, an amazingly strong woman, was stoic. During all this time I had heard her cry only once—when I'd called her from the car a few days earlier to tell her about Cooke's coma. In the aftermath of Cooke's passing, though, she never lost composure. Her strategy for emotional survival served her well.

I wanted to survive. I had survived. But that powerful sensation commonly called "survivor's guilt" was all over me.

Why me?

Why not Cooke?

Why couldn't she have received the gift, the miracle?

God's grace is a miraculous gift for us all. I have held to that belief since I was a young woman.

Now I faced the fact that the nature of that grace—and the nature of that gift—remained mysterious.

I didn't want mysterious. I wanted clarity. I wanted Cooke. I wanted to spend the rest of my life talking to my sister every single night of the week.

At fifty-nine, new life had been given me.

At sixty-four, Cooke was gone.

On the day after my amazing medical procedure, grief overwhelmed celebration, complex confusion overwhelmed simple gratitude.

Mom said that I looked so refreshed it seemed as though I had had a face-lift.

My dear friend Tammy stayed at the hospital with me every day and slept there every night.

The kind of love I received was incredible.

The kind of pain I felt at losing my sister was equally incredible.

Physically, I was whole. Emotionally, I was broken . . . but not sunk.

High Hopes

I stayed in close contact with Eric at OneLegacy. I was eager for news of those who had received Jessica's organs and tissues.

"Here's how it works, Patty," he said. "I cannot give you their phone numbers or addresses. But through our office, you can send them a card. On that card, of course, you're free to write whatever you like."

"I want to meet them. I want them to meet Mama and me. In them, I know we will feel and see my sister's spirit."

"You have a great attitude," said Eric, "and I encourage you to send them all such requests."

"And do you think they'll respond?" I wondered.

"You can never tell. Sometimes they do. Sometimes they don't. But just as I am pledged to protect Jessica's privacy, I am pledged to protect theirs. The decision about whether to meet with you—or even simply respond to your card—is up to them."

"I understand. My hopes are high."

"Then I'd encourage you to put those hopes in your cards. Write whatever is in your heart."

"I will."

"But give it time. This isn't an instant process."

"I'll begin this weekend, Eric. You'll get the cards from me, and before long I expect to be hearing from those who Jessica helped."

"I hope so."

"I know so."

17

THE FIRST MEMORIAL for Cooke was for the family at Forest Lawn, where Kelly and Aunt Bay were buried.

I found the strength to attend, but I was still extremely weak. It's difficult to remember what was said—I was in a fog—but I recall that my cousin Eddie led the prayers. My prayer continued to be "Thank you, God, but . . ."

The "but," of course, had to do with Cooke. Did she have to leave her family so suddenly and so soon?

After the brief service, we got into the limo and went to Chef Marilyn's on Crenshaw Boulevard for old-school soul food. It was good to be with my family, but psychologically I was not in good shape.

I went home and fell into bed. I was done.

Tammy stayed with me at home for another week. Having her there was deeply comforting. I don't know how she did it. She had her own life—her children, her grandchildren, and her dogs, too—and yet she managed to be by my side, making sure I took my medicine, helping me bathe, cooking my meals. What an amazing friend!

Other friends came through as well—Benita, Cecille, Sonia, Star, Denise, Carol, Selene . . . and on and on. My wonderful sisters, Timolin and Casey, stayed with me for several days. Pam was also amazing; she kept it all together. I know it wasn't easy for her; she was also close to Cooke.

I was so blessed to have so many people in my life who sustained me—and continue to do so—with unconditional love.

I will always remember and treasure these sad but special times when we laughed and grieved together.

Despite all the loving support, my emotional condition worsened when in June a second memorial was held for the wide circle of people who had come to love Cooke. John and her children hosted it in their Tarzana home, where I had not been since Mother's Day.

It was another rough day for me. When I entered the

house, I saw a table set up in the foyer with Cooke's picture. It was an old publicity photo from when she had worked as an actress, and she looked stunning, angelic, and excited about the possibilities ahead. The photo broke my heart.

Under the photo was a card that carried the words "Be still and know that I am." I read it as a mysterious mixture of scripture and Cooke's own personal Buddhist-leaning beliefs.

Seeing Cooke's picture and reading that card did me in. I was beyond broken. I spent the entire day weeping.

The memorial was held in the backyard. It was a beautiful day. Butterflies were fluttering. Flowers were blooming. I followed the flight of the butterflies. I smelled the sweetness of the flowers. People read from holy books. Friends told beautiful stories illustrating my sister's charitable heart. Family members spoke of her wisdom, kindness, and sensitivity. And through it all, I sobbed like a baby.

The summer loomed ahead, and though I had been given this miraculous gift, grief continued to overwhelm gratitude.

After the memorial, I went home, fell into bed, and closed my eyes.

Innocent

Jessica's new son, Lucas, went to live with Julio and Julio's family—Julio's mom, sister, and brother. He was a healthy and beautiful baby.

Meanwhile, my life, that much emptier without my sister, went on. I was looking for connections.

OneLegacy had a dinner for the families of donors, and I thought that might help. Arturo and I decided to attend. I wanted to hear what others had gone through. There were so many Hispanic families that the program was conducted in Spanish.

As the evening began, photographs of the donors were projected on a screen.

Jessica—beautiful Jessica—was among them.

The donors were applauded and celebrated.

During the ceremony, we were seated at a table with another Hispanic family. I'm shy and didn't engage them in conversation. But Arturo, always the extrovert, did. The father began telling the story of their fourteen-year-old son, who'd been killed in a car accident. The driver of the car was obviously negligent and guilty of manslaughter. There had been a long and difficult trial. The jury returned with a verdict only a few days before this dinner.

"I knew I would see justice done," said the father.

"Did you?" asked Arturo.

"The driver was found . . ."

The father couldn't get the word out. But it was clear what the word was. Finally, he said it. "Innocent. The driver was found innocent."

Tears were streaming down the father's cheeks. The mother was crying as well. At that point, none of us could hold back tears.

Innocent, I kept thinking to myself.

What does it mean to be innocent?

Wasn't the fourteen-year-old boy innocent?

Wasn't Jessica?

18

CALL IT WHAT you will. Depression. Anxiety. Despair.

I call it the blues. And the blues were all around me. The summer of 2009 was the hardest of my life.

It wasn't the routine of medicines that got to me. God knows I was used to taking meds. It wasn't the aches and pains that come with major surgery. Major surgery had kept me alive and I wasn't about to complain about physical discomfort.

It was my mind, heart, and soul.

I was so far down in the dumps I couldn't see my way back.

Family stayed close by. Friends did all they could to cheer me up. But nothing could raise my spirits.

Cooke was gone.

I never asked God, "Why me?" while I was sick. But when Cooke died, I started asking, "Why me? Why was I the one to be here while she was the one who left?"

I still don't have all the answers to that one.

Tammy and I did a lot of talking during this time. It was pretty much all I could do, since I was told my recuperation would take from four to six months. What kept me from falling apart was the realization that love is a healer, a reviver, and a provider. Love drove and protected my relationships.

I knew that it was all about learning to recognize and accept God's will. I knew that accepting it was a cornerstone of spiritual wisdom.

I knew, I knew, I knew.

But knowing didn't seem to help.

Depression deepened.

Why Cooke?

Why not me?

I couldn't stop obsessing over those questions.

And when the answers didn't come, the blues got bluer.

Responses

OneLegacy called to say that they had received a response to my cards.

"Only one?" I asked.

"Only one," they confirmed.

They forwarded the card, and I eagerly opened it. It was a long and beautiful letter from Natalie Cole describing her deep and genuine gratitude. She went on to say that she would love to meet us and hear all about Jessica.

I had expected other responses from other recipients. They never came. But on this day, at this moment, I felt fulfilled.

And I felt gratitude. I knew that now I'd get to see just how Jessica's story had intersected with Natalie's. I'd get to see the miracle in action.

19

THE BLUES HAVE a life of their own. They don't want to go away. They want to linger and last. They want to keep you in isolation. Stay in bed till noon. Don't leave the house. Mope around all day. Pile up one negative thought atop another. What's the use? What's the point?

I was missing my father, missing my brother, missing my aunt Bay, missing my cousin Janice, missing my soul mate Marvin, missing Rob's nanny, Drue, and mostly missing my precious sister Cooke.

I was missing life. The long hot summer was getting

longer by the day. I was moping around in my depression, doing nothing, getting nowhere.

Then the card arrived.

It was a simple card, but it seemed surrounded by light. Its light broke through my darkness.

The card gave me something I never had before—the name of the woman who gave me her kidney.

Jessica.

The name of her sister writing the note.

Patty.

Two sisters, just like me and Cooke.

The note was short and very sweet.

The note was filled with gratitude—gratitude for the fact that her sister could be of service.

The note was filled with curiosity—curiosity about how I was doing.

The note was filled with humility—if I were unable to meet her family, Patricia would understand.

The note touched my heart.

I didn't think twice. I went to my desk and immediately responded.

"I'm excited to meet you and your family," I wrote. "God bless Jessica for giving me such an extraordinary gift. And God bless you, Patty, for reaching out."

"I'm Scared"

"I understand that you're scared," Arturo said to me. "It's scary to meet a big star like Natalie Cole."

"It isn't that," I said. "I admire artists and I respect their talent, but I don't feel intimidated by them."

"Then why are you scared?"

"It has to do with Jessica."

"Jessica?"

"I want to reconnect with Jessica."

"Well, you will."

"But what if the reconnection isn't there? What if I don't feel anything? What if meeting Natalie is like meeting a stranger?"

"She is a stranger, Patty."

"But she has Jessica. She's living with my sister. She can't be a stranger any more than Jessica was a stranger."

"It's all going to be fine," said Arturo.

"But what if it isn't?" I asked.

I carried the question with me—all summer long.

20

SOMETIMES YOU JUST have to get up. Sometimes it's as simple as getting out of bed. But that one step—from the bed to the floor—can take more effort than climbing Mount Everest.

I started exerting a little effort here and a little effort there. I got out of bed. I called a friend. I called another. I called my voice coach, Seth Riggs. I made an appointment. It had been a long time since I had sung. I needed to get back in shape. I needed my voice, my music, my faith.

My faith had never gone away, but it sure had taken a long vacation. Patty's note helped bring my faith back.

It took a while to arrange the meeting because I didn't

want to go when my spirits were down. I wanted to go when I felt good. I didn't want Patty to see me in despair. I wanted to go in gratitude.

We were to meet at the offices of OneLegacy, the organization that had brought us all together. I asked my manager, Barbara, my cousin Pam, and my dear friend Tammy to accompany me.

"Are you nervous, Natalie?" Tammy asked me on the drive over.

"Sure, I'm nervous. What if they don't like me? What if we have nothing to say to each other? What if the meeting is a bust?"

My Hand

Natalie had arrived before us. She was with her cousin, her friend, and her manager.

Natalie was beaming.

I was beaming

She came right up to me and said, "Patty?"

"Yes," I said. "I'm Patty."

And then we simply hugged each other for a long, long time.

We were both crying. We were both speechless. We both understood the power of the moment.

Natalie introduced us to her friend Tammy. We introduced Natalie to my husband and my mother. Her nurse Esther, my Aunt Tete, embraced her as well.

"I remembered you from Cedars," Esther told Natalie. "You were always so sweet. And then when I saw you on *Larry King*, you were so open and honest about all your problems that my heart said, 'Esther, if you ever have a chance to help this woman, you must.'"

"Thank you so much," said Natalie. "You did it. You really did it."

"It wasn't me," Esther replied. "It was God."

"Before we start talking," I said to Natalie, "I just want to ask you one thing."

"Please," she said.

"May I touch my sister? May I put my hand close to your kidney and feel my sister?"

"Sure!"

I placed my hand on Natalie and left it there. I closed my eyes. I felt the spirit and loving presence of my sister.

She was there.

She was with us.

We were one.

21

I IMMEDIATELY FELL in love with Patty, her mother, Dina, and Patty's husband, Arturo. And of course it was wonderful seeing Nurse Esther. It was a family reunion and I felt honored to be so accepted. These were good, warm, loving people.

We had a lot to talk about. We had stories to share, and from my point of view, I had tremendous gratitude to share. After my long dark summer, light was pouring in.

"When I see you," said Patty, "I see Jessica. I feel her."

"Nothing could make me happier," I said. "Please tell me more about your sister."

In describing Jessica's character, Patty made it clear

why the gift of her kidney was so appropriate to her spirit. What moved me most, though, were Patty's ideas about the transplant phenomenon. She didn't see donating her sister's organs as merely a gesture. She saw it as a way of literally keeping her sister alive.

"Jessica becomes part of you, Natalie," said Patty, "and you become part of her. That's so beautiful. If she had been buried and her body untouched, that would be it. The end. But now she is leading many other lives."

The emotional highlight of the day came when Patty asked to put her hand over her sister's kidney.

Her hand stayed steady against my skin. The connection was real. Sisters connecting with sisters.

Slowly, very slowly, my life returned. Summer was turning to autumn. In a fine moment, I was asked to perform at the Hollywood Bowl in September. Originally, I had been scheduled to play the Bowl in July but had to cancel because of my transplant. It was a truly gracious gesture on the part of the staff to accommodate me.

I realized that it had been nearly a year and a half since I had worked on a regular basis. So I began to prepare diligently. In choosing my music, I thought of Cooke every day. In going back out in the world, I thought of Jessica every day. Both women were going back out there with me.

Cooke would always send me songs and poems, always

make suggestions about what material best suited me. I missed her advice. I missed our nightly calls. I missed her like I have never missed anyone.

At the same time, I was able to comfort myself with a thought that even the devil couldn't dispel: Throughout my life, I freely, openly, and frequently expressed my love to Cooke. Time and again, I told how much I cherished her.

I had said the same thing to my father; to my brother, Kelly; to my husband, Marvin; to my aunt Bay, my cousin Janice, and my dear friend Drue.

I had spoken my heart. They had heard me. They had accepted my love. They had returned my love.

On the deepest level, we had embraced. Even after their passings, I could feel the bond. The bond couldn't be broken. Love had been voiced; love had lasted; love could not die.

Love saved me, renewed me, and sustained me. Love saw me through the blues. Love defeated my depression. Patty's love for Jessica, my love for Cooke, all this love was too strong to be denied.

We all have our stories. I have mine, Cooke has hers, Jessica and Patty theirs. Ultimately, though, I realize that those stories are not of our own making. God is the storyteller. He is the creative king of kings. He sets us out on a path. Afraid or uncertain, we believe that by grabbing control over every event in our lives, we can direct our own paths. That's an illusion. Perhaps we have control for an hour or a day, but here comes the storm, here comes the tidal wave of circumstances that knocks us to the ground. Bad fortune comes on the heels of good. Or vice versa. A birth. A death. A sickness. A cure. Questions without answers. Answers that don't make sense. Mysteries without solutions.

All we know is that the God of love is shrouded in mystery. We cannot see Him. We cannot hear His literal voice. We invoke His spirit by living out His message—to love always, to love extravagantly, to love even those who wish us harm. It is a challenging, difficult, radical love.

But by living such love, we guarantee ourselves peace within. Our losses become our gains. Cooke is gone, but Patty is here. To know a deeper grief is to know a more profound love.

I am not a singer who often suffers from stage fright, but the night of my Hollywood Bowl concert, I was a nervous wreck! Built on the side of a huge hill, the Bowl, with its enormous seating capacity of seventeen thousand, is awesome. It breathes history. It brings back memories of my dad. For me, it's one of the great venues—a magical place.

Waiting to go onstage, I was worried about so many things: Would I have the strength to sing a complete concert? Would my voice be there? Would my poise?

I missed Cooke more than ever. Her absence was glaring. I needed to pray. I needed her laugh, her smile, anything to hold on to. I needed to remember and feel Cooke's presence.

I was hyperventilating and laughing at myself at the same time.

Fortunately, my medical team was there, right by my side, along with my friends and family—all out in force to cheer me on.

When I finally made the move and walked out on the stage of the Hollywood Bowl, it was one of the biggest steps of my life. I didn't know if my fans would respond. I didn't know whether I could do what I had done before.

By the time I started singing, though, I felt pretty damn good. I looked great. My confidence came back. I could hear the audience clapping and hooting in anticipation. It was a full house—and I was feeling full, too.

I sang "The Very Thought of You"—and thought of you, Dad; of you, Cooke; of you, Kelly and Drue and Bay and Janice—with a depth of feeling I had never experienced before. The past two years had tried my spirit—and my spirit, with the help of family and friends, had made it through.

The concert was a success, even a triumph. It was a rockin' night. I sang and sang and sang. The audience rose to their feet. They were applauding me, but I also felt them applauding Cooke and Jessica. Cooke was there in spirit; Jessica was there in the flesh.

22

THIS STORY TOOK place over a two-year period. That's not very long, but in those brief, intense months I learned some of my greatest lessons.

One. Life is real and so is God. He is the true storyteller in our lives. You only think you run your life. You don't.

Two. No days are promised us. None. Zero. Nada. So—and this isn't easy—we must learn to make them *all* count.

Three. Bad things happen. Don't waste your time asking, "Why me?" Most of the time it isn't even about you. So get over it. Instead, ask what this experience can teach you.

Four. Attitude is everything. To spend one's day bitching and moaning, playing the victim and singing the "poor me" song is the rudest, most insulting thing you can do to your Creator. If God and love seem very far away from you, guess who moved?

Five. The value of friends and laughter is priceless. Life is tough enough. There may be many things you will never have. But if you can have one of these—friends or laughter—you will have the other as well.

Throughout my life, I have frequently and freely expressed my love to my family, to my friends, to all my loved ones.

They know how much I cherish them.

They accepted and embraced my love, imperfect as it is, and they returned it tenfold. It is the kind of love too strong to be denied.

There are so many things in this world that I don't know or understand. But I do know this in the core of my being:

It was love that sustained and lifted me during a fragile and frightening time in my life. Love led me when I couldn't see my way out. Love carried me when I couldn't take another step. When my hunger was insatiable, love fed and filled me. Love comforted me when I was sick and hurting. Love kept me sane, focused, and steady—all day long, all night through.

Love brought me back.

Acknowledgments

NATALIE

It is with a full heart that I thank the people who gave me the hope and strength to see me through these past two years. I pray that I will not leave anyone off this list.

First and most important, Mom, Rob, Casey, Timolin, Harleigh, Sage, Jen, Barba, Eddie Cole and family, Kearney and Marie, Julian, Justin, Wyatt, Caroline, Johnny, Veronica, Carter, Pamela, Tammy, Benita, Cecille, V, Reyna, and my incredible touring family of musicians and crew . . . love you, love you, love you.

I'm blessed to say that the rest of this list is too long to mention. So to those who've been there for me, you are beautiful, and I thank God for your presence in my life.

When things looked pretty bad, your support and prayers changed everything; your love brought me back.

I'd also like to acknowledge the wonderful doctors and hospitals that saw me through this crisis: Dr. Joel Mittleman; Dr. Graham Woolf; Dr. Maurice Levy; Dr. Louis Cohen; Dr. Tara Timmerman; Dr. Angelo Acquista; Dr. Susan Karimi; Cedars-Sinai Medical Center; Tarzana Medical Center; OneLegacy, for their amazing work; Ken Thiry, president and CEO of DaVita, Inc., Dialysis Centers (special thanks to the staff in Beverly Hills); and the various dialysis centers throughout the world that were fantastic, in Milan, Manila, Istanbul, and the London Clinic. Also, Ken Kleinberg, CEO, University Kidney Research Organization, and his staff—dedicated and delightful.

I'm grateful to my professional advisors: Barbara Rose, kick-butt-in-the-boardroom manager, confidante, and great girlfriend. The William Morris Endeavor Agency: David Snyder, Chris Burke, Rob Heller, and Ben Bernstein—love you guys. Ron Stern and Sissy Alexander, with Designer Travel—just the best! Stuart Fried and Jonathan Ehrlich, partners at Grubman, Indursky and Shire. Howard Grossman, senior partner, WG&S Business and Wealth Management, not your typical business manager, but also a mentor, brother from another mother, and friend.

David Ritz, cowriter, cocollaborator, coconspirator. The patience of Job and a delight to work with.

For more information on kidney research: www.UKROCharity.org. And for organ donations: www.OneLegacy.org.

DAVID

Thanks to:

Natalie, whose brilliance—in music, mind, and spirit—transformed our collaboration into a beautiful blessing.

Patty and Arturo Argueta, for their deeply soulful sharing.

My loving family: Roberta, Alison, Jessica, Henry, Jim, Charlotte, Nino, James, Issac, Pops, Esther, Elizabeth, and all my great nephews and nieces.

The publishing folk: David (the Rainmaker) Vigliano, David Rosenthal, Bob Bender, Johanna Li.

My loving loyal friends: Alan Eisenstock, Harry Weinger, Herb Powell, Richard Freed, Richard Cohen.

The hip cats without whom I'd be lost: Skip, Dennis, Dejon, Juan, Ian, John, Tom.

Appendix

THE FOUR AGREEMENTS

COOKE PASSED THESE four principles on to me. As I was adding them to the book, I realized that she'd sent them to me on her birthday!

I was quite taken with how four simple sentences, developed by Don Miguel Ruiz in his book *The Four Agreements,* could carry so much weight, be so inspiring and powerful, and drive me crazy trying to live them.

1. Be impeccable with my words.
2. Don't take anything personally.
3. Don't make assumptions.
4. Always do my best.

Printed in the United States
By Bookmasters